IMAGES
of England

EXETER CITY
FOOTBALL CLUB
1904-1994

At Last! If (as you must) you discount the championship of the East Devon Senior League in 1904/05, their inaugural season, Exeter City's first title arrived in 1989/90 when Terry Cooper's team won the Fourth Division title, having beaten Scarborough 3-2 at home on 28 April. Three days later, in front of 7,544 ecstatic fans at St James's Park, the trophy was presented to the club before the game with Burnley – which Exeter won 2-1. The picture shows manager Terry Cooper being carried off the pitch. The City players, from left to right: Dave Walter, Richard Young, Shaun Taylor, Brian McDermott and Lee Rogers.

IMAGES
of England

EXETER CITY
FOOTBALL CLUB
1904-1994

Compiled by
Dave Fisher and Gerald Gosling

TEMPUS

First published 1998
Copyright © Dave Fisher and Gerald Gosling, 1998

Tempus Publishing Limited
The Mill, Brimscombe Port,
Stroud, Gloucestershire, GL5 2QG

ISBN 0 7524 1167 5

Typesetting and origination by
Tempus Publishing Limited
Printed in Great Britain by
Midway Clark Printing, Wiltshire

Present and forthcoming titles from Tempus Publishing:

Bury Football Club
Cardiff City Football Club 1899-1947
Cardiff City Football Club 1947-1971
Charlton Athletic Football Club
Crystal Palace Football Club
Gillingham Football Club
Newport County Football Club 1912-1960
Oxford United Football Club
Plymouth Argyle Football Club 1886-1986
Reading Football Club 1871-1997
Sheffield United Football Club
Swansea Town Football Club 1912-1964
Sunderland Football Club
Tranmere Rovers Football Club
York City Football Club

Contents

BACK ROW.—S. Greenway (*Trainer*)　Messrs. A. Norman Kendall　A. Chadwick (*Manager*)　J. J. Pengelly　W. Norman　G. A. Middleweek　S. H. Thomas (*Secretary*)
THIRD ROW.—E. Lewis　R. Loram　R. Gerrish　W. Kirby　R. Pym　S. Strettle　A. Evans　F. Hunt　J. Manaton　— (*Groundsman*)
SECOND ROW.—F. Whittaker　J. Fort　J. Rigby　Mr. M. J. McGahey (*Chairman*)　W. Smith　F. Marshall　H. McCann　J. C. Lee
FRONT ROW.—H. Holt　C. Pratt　F. Lovett　J. Lagan　H. Orr　J. Goddard

Photo. by S. A. Chandler & Co., Arcade Studio, Arcade, Exeter

EXETER CITY F.C.

Exeter City 1913/14. From left to right, back row: S. Greenway (Trainer), Mr A. Norman Kendall, Mr Arthur Chadwick (Manager), Mr J. Pengelly, Mr W. Norman, Mr G.A. Middleweek, Mr S.H. Thomas (Secretary). Third row: E. Lewis, R. Loram, R. Gerrish, W. Kirby, R. Pym, S. Strettle, A. Evans, F. Hunt, J. Manaton, -?- (Groundsman). Second row: F. Whittaker, J. Fort, J. Rigby, Mr M.J. McGahey (Chairman), W. Smith, F. Marshall, H. McCann, J.C. Lee. Front row: H. Holt, C. Pratt, F. Lovett, J. Lagan, H. Orr, J. Goddard.

Introduction

What a joy! Page after page that will bring the memories flooding back for the dedicated football fans and the less committed alike. This book really brings home the old saying 'A picture is worth a thousand words' as we step back into a time when footballs were leather and every Exeter City fan wore a red-and-white scarf. These archive photographs are like old friends at Christmas – not really appreciated until they are dusted off and those introductions made all over again.

When looking through these pictures, recollections start flowing back: I was so old when that goal was scored, I was working there when he was playing, even my grandfather doesn't remember him. Whether you read this amazing collection from cover to cover, or just dip into it where the pages fall open, you cannot help but find a memory to warm the heart.

Exeter City may not have enjoyed the most successful of histories, but the club has certainly provided some glorious moments – many of which are captured in the following pages.

Jerry Charge
Sports Editor, *Express & Echo*
February 1998.

Foreword

As you turn the pages of this book you soon realise what a rich history Exeter City Football Club has. They may not have been one of the most successful clubs since becoming a Football League side in 1920, but they have certainly brought a good deal of pleasure (and heartache) to thousands of supporters.

The club is very much part of the local community and this was admirably demonstrated when supporters and businesses rallied round during the club's hour of need 1995, when the very existence of The Grecians was under threat. Fund-raising events were organized, such as street bucket collections, and trust groups were formed: all played their part in winning the battle to keep the Football League flag flying in the City of Exeter.

The county of Devon has long been regarded by many as being a sleepy backwater, miles from anywhere, and not really a football area. How wrong they can be! I quickly found out on my move from Stoke City in July 1993 that these preconceptions are totally inaccurate (apart from the long journeys). Once I had settled into the Exeter area, I came to realise what a superb part of the world it is to live in, and many players will tell you exactly the same thing. It is persuading people to come here in the first place that often proves difficult.

The support for the club is quite brilliant. Just compare attendances at games involving other Division Three clubs, and you will see just how much football means to so many people in Exeter and the surrounding areas. As a player or manager, upon arriving at the club, you soon realise just how passionate the supporters are – especially at local derbies. They care as much about those games as fans would in Manchester, Liverpool or London.

The top level of the game in the late 1990s is covered in so much detail that clubs like Exeter City are sometimes ignored and taken for granted. But I know from experience, since becoming manager in July 1995, that The Grecians mean just as much to the people in this area. It is their club and forms part of the real grass roots of professional football.

The history of Exeter City Football Club has been painstakingly recorded by a handful of enthusiasts so that future generations of supporters are reminded of the club's glorious (and sometimes not so glorious) past. It has not been an easy journey through history, with many tales of the club battling against the odds and teetering on the brink of financial disaster. But the triumphs that have come The Grecians' way have been earned by hard work and appreciated all the more when they have occurred.

This photographic record of the club, compiled by David Fisher and Gerald Gosling, will, I am sure, prove a fitting tribute to all those who have played their part in keeping the name of Exeter City FC to the fore and be a superb reference book for many years to come. This collection of photographs is a fascinating record of past teams, players and events. It is more than just a football book though, for it is also a social record of how the game has changed over the years. Take a look at the kit worn by the players, the seemingly compulsory headgear of supporters in the days before the Second World War and the way in which pre-1939 footballers always look so hard and mean.

I am sure you will find this book as interesting as I have done. I am proud to have played a small part in the overall history of Exeter City FC and honoured to have been asked to write this forward. I sincerely hope that Exeter City will continue to bring pleasure to people for many years to come.

Peter Fox
1998

One

The Early Years

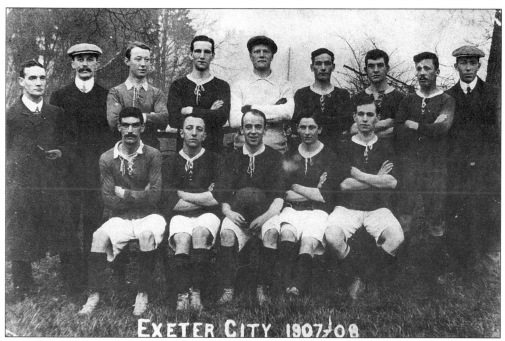

One of the earliest pictures of Exeter City, taken in the 1907/08 season when they were wearing green shirts and white shorts. Legend has it that they changed to their red and white colours because green is considered unlucky for the team that wears it, although Glasgow Celtic seem to prove this to be incorrect. From left to right, back row: Mr C. Fey, Mr W. Bastin, E. Eveleigh, H. Dyer, W. Wells, S. Bastin, P. Warner, R. Mould, Mr S.H. Thomas (Secretary). Front: B. Massey, R. Fenwick, J. Sellick, H. Singlehurst, W. Letheren.

Crowd scenes can sometimes be a little boring as they are often repetitive, but the authors make no apologies for including some from City's early years here. They are invaluable for showing the buildings and terraces around St James's Park and how little, or how much, they have changed. Above: A Southern League game with Plymouth Argyle, around 1909. In this picture, the stand that burnt down on 17 November 1925 can be seen. Of special interest is the manner in which the stanchion has been padded in a rugby-post fashion. Below: Fans standing where 'The Cowshed' is situated today, during a Plymouth League game between Exeter Reserves and 107th RGA in 1910. It must have been a cold day – most of the men are well-buttoned up.

Above: Another reserve game, this time in 1909/10 against Torquay United, who also played in the Plymouth & District League. The crash barriers may not meet with today's stringent safety regulations. Below: in the same game, the stand looks less than full. But what about the magnificent (there is no other word for them) hats the ladies are wearing?

Very little is known about this picture, except that it is of Exeter City playing Plymouth Argyle at Home Park in around 1913. City first played Argyle on 11 November 1908 in their first season in the Southern League. The game was at St James's Park where 7,000 people saw Jimmy Bell score both Exeter goals in a 2-1 win. However, The Pilgrims took early revenge beating Exeter 2-0 in an FA Cup Second Round game at Home Park the following February and then winning the return League game, a month later, 4-0.

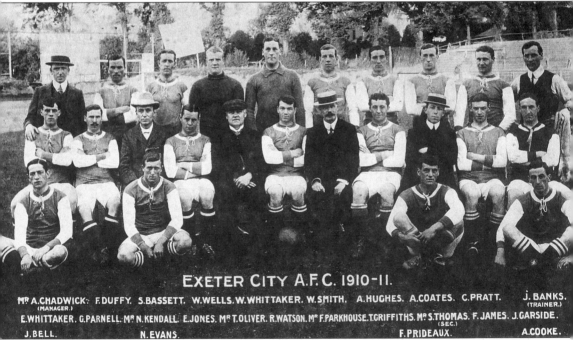

EXETER CITY A.F.C. 1910-11.

Mᴿ A.CHADWICK. F.DUFFY. S.BASSETT. W.WELLS. W.WHITTAKER. W.SMITH. A.HUGHES. A.COATES. C.PRATT. J. BANKS.
(MANAGER.) (TRAINER.)
E.WHITTAKER. G.PARNELL. Mᴿ N.KENDALL. E.JONES. Mᴿ T.OLIVER. R.WATSON. Mᴿ F.PARKHOUSE. T.GRIFFITHS. Mᴿˢ S.THOMAS. F. JAMES. J.GARSIDE.
(SEC.)
J.BELL. N.EVANS. F.PRIDEAUX. A.COOKE.

Exeter City at the start of the 1910/11 season taken on the Big Bank at St James's Park. From left to right, back row: Arthur Chadwick (Manager), F. Duffy, Spencer Bassett, W. Wells, Walter Whittaker, William Smith, Archibald Hughes, Arthur Coates, C. Pratt, J. Banks (Trainer). Middle row: Enos Whittaker, G. Parnell, N. Kendall, Edwin Jones, Mr T. Oliver, Bob Watson, Mr F. Parkhouse, Thomas Griffiths, Mr S.H. Thomas (Secretary), Francis James, James Garside. Front row: James Bell, Nolan Evans, Fred Prideaux, Arthur Cooke.

'Bob' Watson was a popular inside right who played 156 League and cup games for Exeter City between 1908 and 1912. He was the club's first professional skipper and played for Middlesbrough (his home town), Woolwich Arsenal and Leeds before joining Exeter. He later moved on to Stalybridge Celtic. This picture was the forty-ninth in Gallaher's cigarette cards series *Association Football Club Colours* covering the 1909/10 season. It describes City as 'a club of recent formation... they obtained admission to the First Division of the Southern League in 1908 and have enjoyed two fairly good seasons'.

Exeter City 1911/12 season. From left to right, back row: Enos Whittaker, Nolan Evans, Arthur Rutter, Arthur Coates, Fred Prideaux, Frank Cornan, J. Banks (Trainer). Middle row: G. Parnell, Spencer Bassett, Arthur Chadwick (Manager), Thomas Griffiths, James Garside. Front row: Henry Lockett, John Fort. Whether 'Laddie' was the club mascot or belonged to one of the players is not known.

GALLAHER'S CIGARETTES.

"BOB" WATSON, EXETER CITY, 1909-10.

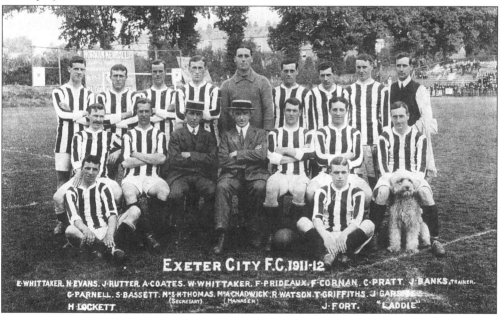

EXETER CITY F.C. 1911-12
E. WHITTAKER. N. EVANS. J. RUTTER. A. COATES. W. WHITTAKER. F. PRIDEAUX. F. CORNAN. C. PRATT. J. BANKS, TRAINER.
G. PARNELL. S. BASSETT. Mrs H. THOMAS. Mr A. CHADWICK. R. WATSON. T. GRIFFITHS. J. GARSIDE.
(SECRETARY) (MANAGER)
H. LOCKETT J. FORT. "LADDIE"

The programme for the Exeter City against Swindon game at the end of the 1910/11 season. Swindon came to St James's Park already crowned as Southern League champions but lost 2-1, City's goals coming from Francis James in his last game for the club before moving to Coventry. But it was not a case of Swindon relaxing: they had the matter of revenge to consider, having lost 1-0 at home to Exeter on Christmas Eve – their only home defeat that season. Despite the double over the champions, Exeter finished down in thirteenth place in the Southern League.

City's Edwardian programmes were by no means modest affairs: this one stretched to ten pages – many more than the programmes on sale at St James Park between the wars and only two less than those printed in the 1940s and 1950s. Some of the advertisements are wonderfully evocative of the period and the prices that existed before modern inflation. A 'Dunn's Famous Felt Hat' could be bought for 3/9d (about 19p) and three collars cost a shilling (5p) at Norton's Needlework Depot in Sidwell Street; new watches could be purchased from five shillings (25p) and new clocks from a shilling at Sidney Herbert's, also in Sidwell street. Herbert would *give* you a half-dozen tea spoons and a pair of sugar tongs if you bought your wedding ring from his shop. Several shops advertised Truman's Genuine Oatmeal Stout (strongly recommended for invalids) at 2/6d per dozen pints (one new penny a pint). Those were the days – if City lost you could drown your sorrows in style.

E. CROMPTON

EXETER CITY

Ellis Crompton was one of several experienced players whom Arthur Chadwick tempted to the West Country and Southern League football. He had played for Blackburn Rovers and Tottenham Hotspur and it was no coincidence that when he first played for, and captained, Exeter in 1912/13 they jumped from fifteenth to seventh in the Southern League table. Crompton moved to Bristol Rovers for a fee of £400 the following season but returned to St James Park, playing 156 more games between 1921 and 1926. An inside forward in that one season before the First World War, he transferred to the half line where he astonished opponents with his speed and agility, despite nearing forty. He moved to Barnstaple Town in 1926.

Twenty-seven days after the end of the 1913/14 season, Exeter City departed from Southampton on what, for such a small club at that time, was an astounding tour of South America. The Southern League had been asked to recommend a club that would be representative of a typical English football side and they chose Exeter City. Around twenty directors and players made the trip and, if this picture that shows most of them finding their sea-legs, a day or two out from Southampton, is to be believed, some wives went as well.

The palm trees suggest an away game at Torquay. It is, in fact, during the last match of City's eight-game South American tour, when they drew 3-3 with Brazil. Imagine the headlines today if England could manage that.

The caption from this picture reads 'Eis o XI do Exter [sic] City, da Inglaterra, o primeiro quadro profissional que jogou no Brasil' or, as the erdite reader will know, 'Exeter City from England, the first professional team, to play in Brazil'.

City lost the first game of the tour 1-0 against Argentino Norte (North Argentine) which was virtually the national side. They followed this with wins over Argentine South (3-0), Racing Club de Buenos Aires – the Argentinian champions – (2-0), Rosarian League (3-1), Combinadoes (5-0), Rio de Janeiro (3-0) and Fluminense (5-3). The tour ended with the 3-3 draw against Brazil. The trip contained many exciting moments, notably during the game against Racing Club de Buenos Aires when the home secretary drew his pistol and opened fire on the referee after one of Exeter's goals. We all know the feeling Mr Secretary!

Keepsake from City's 1914 Argentina visit

JUNE 85

Lynn Trout of Topsham Youth Club and the historic football destined for Exeter City's showcase. Picture: JOHN FFOULKES

NOT ANY OLD LEATHER!

EXETER City Football Club is all set to buy a legendary piece of its history — an ancient Argentinian football.

The leather ball was used in an historic match in Argentina in 1914 between City and the Argentinian club Racing. When Exeter won, the Argentinian club secretary was reputedly so angry that he tried to shoot the referee . . .

Mr Dick "Pincher" Pym, 92, of Topsham, a former England international, played in the game and for 71 years he held on to the ball signed by all the Argentinian and Exeter players — as a keepsake.

But this week he offered the ball to Topsham Youth Club to auction to raise much-needed funds — and that is where Exeter City stepped in.

The club felt the ball was a vital part of their history and they offered the Youth Club £100 for it.

EXCLUSIVE

By LARAINE HEMINGWAY

"I feel it is a bit of history that belongs with the club. We had to have it," said City chairman Mr Byron Snell. "I think it is a wonderful thing for it to turn up after all this time. We would like to put it on show at St James's Park."

And the Topsham Youth Club is "over the moon."

"We badly need the money," said Lynn Trout for the club. "I never quite believed a piece of old leather could be worth so much."

Byron Snell will hand over the £100 cheque for the ball at Topsham Youth Club midsummer fete on Saturday.

Exeter is thought to have been the first British club ever to visit Argentina to play football — and rumour has it it took them six weeks to get there.

Mr Pym, new president of

DICK PYM — played in historic game.

Topsham Town Football Club, tells the tale of two shots being fired at the referee by the Racing Club secretary — whereupon both teams turned tail and headed for the dressing room. "They stayed there for some time until the all-clear was given," he said.

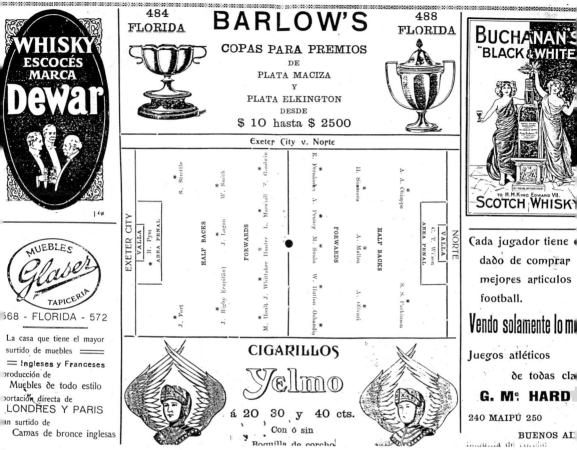

Argentine North versus Exeter City on 14 June 1914. There was still plenty of excitement for the Exeter City party after leaving South America. They went back home on the 18,000 ton *Alcantare* via Lisbon and arrived at Liverpool on 9 August, when Great Britain had been at war with Germany for five days. Not all that long out of Lisbon, their ship was approached by *HMS Vindictive* and had warning shops fired across its bows. They were stopped and identified but not long afterwards a French naval ship fired shots and again stopped them. It would be forty-seven years before Exeter City again played against a South American team: the Bolivian side C.A.R. La Paz played a friendly at St James's Park on 26 October 1961.

Opposite: Dick Pym, Exeter's legendary goalkeeper, who kept the match ball after the game against Racing Club, recalled the incident in an article in the *Express & Echo* in June 1985. The ball eventually went to Exeter City. Another story from the tour, with an apocryphal touch to it, is that a parrot was presented to the Exeter players and they brought it back to England (quarantine regulations?) where it soon died in the colder air. Polly was buried near the St James's Road End goal and City's supply of goals promptly dried up, not to return until the parrot was reburied near the centre spot. Sorry to spoil a good story, but Exeter did score fairly well in 1914/15 – including seven against Southend. In any case it would have been better to have had the bird stuffed: Dick Pym could have taken it with him from goal to goal as a mascot and then the opposition would not have scored!

Dick Pym, universally known as 'Pincher', shares with Cliff Bastin the claim to be the most famous footballer Exeter City produced. Born at nearby Topsham on 2 February 1893, he joined Exeter and played in the reserves towards the end of 1911. He was soon in the first team, making his debut the following year against Stoke on 23 March in front of 4,000 fans at St James's Park. City drew 1-1 but, although the crowd at the game could not have been anything other than impressed with the new goalkeeper, few could have seen the honours that would crowd in on him in the years ahead. In all he played 209 cup and league games for City between 1912 and 1921, including 186 in a row – a run which saw him play in every league game during the three seasons from 1912/13 to 1914/15 and again in 1919/20 when football resumed after the war. He was transferred to Bolton Wanderers at the end of the 1920/21 season for the, then considerable, sum of nearly £5,000. During his stay with the Lancashire club, he played in three FA Cup finals (1923, 1926 and 1929). Bolton won all three and Pym did not concede a goal in any of them. He was also capped three times for England. Pym retired to Topsham where rumour has him playing for the local team when aged forty – at centre forward! A fisherman by trade, he would have starved if his fishing nets had been as empty as his goal nets usually were.

20

Two

Between the Wars

EXETER CITY A.F.C. 1919-1920

Mr S.HEAD. S.STRETTLE. W.GOODWIN. J.MITTON. W.LOVETT. Mr A.G.CHAMBERLAIN. Mr F.PARKHOUSE. S.POPPLEWELL. P.OLDACRE. J.DOCKRAY. Mr S.M.THOMAS.
W.GILL. J.MAKIN. J.COLEBURNE. J.RIGBY. Mr M.J.McGAHEY. R.H.PYM. A.CRAWSHAW. A.GREEN. G.B.POTTER.
E.CONNOR. G.PRATT. C.LINCOLN. H.GREENWAY.

The 1919/20 season was Exeter City's last in the Southern League. At the end of it, along with the rest of the Southern League's First Division, they became founder members of Division Three. Exeter, who finished tenth that season, played their last Southern League at Merthyr Town on 1 May 1920, winning 3-0. The players and staff are pictured at the start of the season in front of the stand. From left to right, back row: Mr S. Head (Director), S. Strettle, William Goodwin, J. Mitton, William Lovett, Mr A.G. Chamberlain (Director), Mr F. Parkhouse (Director), Stan Popplewell, Percival Oldacre, John Dockray, Mr Syd Thomas (Secretary). Middle row: W. Gill, James Makin, Joe Coleburne, James Rigby, Mr M.J. McGahey (Chairman), Dick Pym, A. Crawshaw, Alfred Green, B. Potter. Front row: Edwin Connor, G. Pratt (Trainer), Charles Lincoln, H. Greenway (Groundsman).

EXETER CITY v. BRENTFORD

GHT   EXETER   LEFT

1 – Pym

2 – Coleburne   3 – Feebury

4 – Crawshaw   5 – Carrick   6 – Mitton

Appleton   8 – Makin   9 – Wright   10 – Vowles   11 – Dockray

REFEREE-

Mr. W. H. Richards
Merthyr Vaie

Linesmen- .

13 – Mr. W. J. Bown
Wells

14 – Mr C. J. Pound
Plymouth

Henery   16 – Morley   17 – Boyne   18 – Thompson   19 – Smith

20 – Amos   21 – Elliott   22 – Morris

23 – Rosier   24 – Hodson

25 – Young

FT   BRENTFORD   RIGHT

N.B. —Should any alteration be made in the Officials or Teams at the last moment, a
d will be sent round the Ground notifying the corrected names opposite the numbers
sponding with those on the Programme.

Exeter City began their life as a League side on 28 August 1920, when Brentford visited St James Park and lost 3-0. Exeter scored through William Wright, Charlie Vowles and a John Feebury penalty. It is interesting to note that between the two World Wars, spectators were informed of team changes by 'a board sent round the Ground notifying the corrected names opposite the numbers corresponding with those on the programme'. There was no need for the board at this game as far as the Exeter were concerned – the men named on this programme were those who played.

The players and directors for the 1920/21 season pose at St James's Park. The tall poles at the back were probably erected to hang nets from in an attempt to prevent balls being kicked out of the ground. From left to right, back row: C. Pratt (Trainer), P. Hilton, C. Vowles, J. Isherwood, Mr W. Norman (Director), W. Lakin, Mr F. Parkhouse (Director), J. Mitton, Mr E. Head (Director), J. Feebury, Mr A.H. Chamberlain (Director), R. Pym, L. Appleton, W. Lowton, H. Greenway (Groundsman). Middle row: A. Crawshaw, J. Makin, J. Coleburne, A. Green, Mr M.J. McGahey (Chairman), W. Wright, W. Brayshaw, Arthur Chadwick (Manager), Syd Thomas (Secretary), J. Dockray. Front row: T. Hesmondalgh, W. Betteridge, G. Taylor, T. McIntyre, R. Pollard, J. Carrick, R. Kelland, S. Etherington.

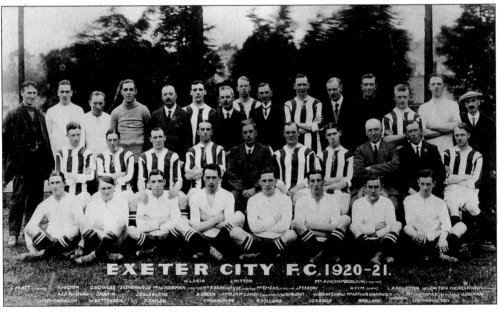

EXETER CITY F.C. 1920-21.

John Dockray played for Exeter City in the 1914/15 season and from the end of the First World War until 1924. He arrived at St James's Park via his native Carlisle and Bury and quickly became a great favourite with the fans. He was twice chosen to represent the Southern League in their annual game with the Welsh League and, in all, played 209 games for City. He fell out with the club and moved to Bideford in 1924.

Exeter City did not prosper in their early years in Division Three, finishing nineteenth, twenty-first, twentieth and sixteenth in the first four seasons. But, under new manager Fred Mavin, who arrived in January 1923, they were to rise to seventh at the end of the 1924/25 season. This picture is of Exeter City in the mid-1920s. The identity of the trophy they are proudly showing is not known.

Arthur Chadwick was Exeter City's first professional manager, having been appointed in 1908 when the decision was made to become a professional club and enter the Southern League. His first job title was 'adviser' but he was manager in all but name. To this day he is the club's longest-serving manager, retiring in 1922 after fourteen years' service. He arrived at St James's Park with a big reputation, having played for Burton Swifts, Southampton, Portsmouth and Northampton Town and won two England caps in 1900. Chadwick made good use of the many contacts in the game that his experience brought. Sadly, for the club and the manager, Exeter City's low financial standing forced him to sell many players, including Dick Pym. He died in 1936 whilst watching a game from the grandstand at St James's Park

Disaster struck St James's Park on Tuesday 17 November 1925 when a fire broke out in the boiler room. It quickly spread and consumed much of the grandstand as well the club's and the players' equipment and most of the paperwork and accounts. The following Saturday, the team travelled to Aberdare for a Division Three game and lost 5-0. The loss of their favourite boots would hardly have put the City players in a happy frame of mind, but Aberdare did play well. Less than two weeks after the fire, Exeter City staged an FA Cup First Round game with Swansea Town. The Welsh side, despite having to put up with changing in a tent, won 3-1.

Just hours after William Compton had scored the only goal of the game to give the City a win against Norwich at Carrow Road on 14 March 1925, the team were heading across the North Sea to the Hook of Holland and a friendly game with the Dutch side Ajax. The Grecians won 5-1 before a big crowd. The touring party are seen here in a cafe in Amsterdam.

Exeter City, 1926/27. From left to right, back row: Mr J. Pengelly (Director), -?-, Mr E. Head (Director), Oswald Randall, Robert Pollard, -?-, Mr Saunders (Director), Mr Nichols (Director), Mr Syd Thomas (Secretary). Third row: -?-, Alexander Pool, -?-, -?-, Albert Potter, Billy McDevitt (Player/Manager), Charlie Miller, Wilf Lowton, -?-, Mr Parkhouse (Director). Second row: -?-. John Garrett, George Purcell, Harold Blackmore, Stan Charlton, Mr M.J. McGahey (Chairman), Arthur Phoenix, Fred Dent, John Ditchburn, Harold Houghton, -?-. Front row: Tom Parkin, Frank Newman, James Walker, William Compton.

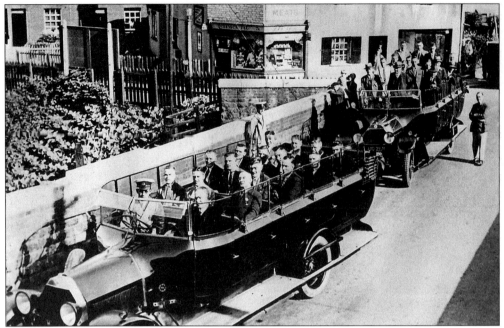

This is not the players and directors about to depart for an away game but the club's annual outing just prior to departure from St James's Park, probably in 1929.

Fred Mavin stayed four years at St James's Park as manager; David Wilson came and stayed less than a year and was followed by Billy McDevitt, who had joined City as a player from Liverpool in 1925. He played for one more season before devoting his considerable energies into being, arguably, Exeter City's best-ever manager. Prior to his appointment, the club had finished twentieth (1925/26), twelfth, eighth and twenty-first. During his years with City, the club underwent considerable improvement, with the great FA Cup run of 1930/31 (of which more later) and a runners-up place in Division Three (South) in 1932/33. Billy McDevitt, as player/manager, can be seen in this 1929/30 picture of the staff and board of the club. He is in the front row with the ball

Exeter City special football trams, 28 September 1929. This was the day that City beat Fulham 2-1 at St James's Park. The message on the reverse of this card reads 'Note thro' ones to Dunsford Road waiting at Elmside'.

All that is known about this *Western Morning News* photograph is that Harry Gee is the Exeter City forward on the ground during an attack on the St James's Road End goal in a game against unknown opposition. Gee was one of the last men Fred Mavin brought to St James's Park at the start of the 1927/28 season. He came from New Brighton and, after thirty-five games for City, he retired, following the 2-2 home draw with Gillingham on 7 April 1928.

The 1930/31 season will be always remembered as 'Exeter City's Cup Year'. They became the first side from Division Three to go into the hat for the Semi-final draw of the FA Cup, albeit as 'Sunderland or Exeter City'. Just before the cup run began – in the unlikely surroundings of Northfleet United's tiny ground – Exeter travelled to meet Clapton (now Leyton) Orient in a Division Three (South) game. They won 3-2 with Arthur Doncaster, Billy Armfield and Percy Varco the marksmen. City, who were to win the return at St James's Park in April 6-1, played the team given in the programme. This mentions, in the aptly named *Oriental Notes*, the fire at St James's Park in 1925 (see p. 24). It describes how '...when the grandstand was badly damaged by fire' the devastation was rectified 'by means of a plucky scheme of subscriptions by Bonds and instalments for payments [...and...] the trouble was dealt with and such improvements made [...that...] the club now possesses one of the most comfortable and well arranged suites of dressing rooms, gymnasiums and offices in the Third Division'.

THE FOOTBALL LEAGUE.

Clapton Orient *v.* Exeter City.

CLAPTON ORIENT.

Colours—White Shirts with Red V, Black Knickers.

Goal

1 Wood

Backs

2 Morley   3 Evans

Half-Backs

4 Broadbent   5 Edmonds   6 Bolton

Forwards
Centre

Right Wing   *Left Wing*

7 Ames   8 Cropper   9 Sanders   10 Fowler   11 Townley

Referee ⭕ Mr. C. F. MOON.

Forwards
Centre

Left Wing   *Right Wing*

12 Doncaster   13 Houghton   14 Varco   15 Purcell   16 Armfield

Half-Backs

17 Barber   18 Dennington   19 Clarke

Backs

20 Miller   21 Baugh

Goal

22 Jones

EXETER CITY.

Colours—Red & White Striped Shirts, Blue Knickers.

Linesmen—Messrs. W. E. WOOD (Red) and F. RATCLIFF (Blue)

Alterations in the above teams will be notified on board

The Football League. Results to October 18th (inclusive).	Pld.	Won	Drn.	Lost	For	Agst.	Pts.
Notts County	12	10	2	0	36	9	22
Northampton Town ...	11	7	3	1	17	5	17
Torquay United	12	7	2	3	34	21	16
Brentford	12	5	4	3	22	18	14
Crystal Palace	11	5	3	3	33	20	13
Coventry City	11	5	3	3	25	15	13
Fulham	11	5	3	3	18	20	13
Gillingham	11	4	4	3	21	14	12
Southend United ...	11	5	2	4	26	22	12
Bournemouth & B.A. ...	11	4	4	3	19	17	12
Swindon Town ...	12	6	0	6	26	24	12
Watford	11	5	2	4	18	18	12
Brighton & Hove Albion	12	4	4	4	15	15	12
Exeter City	12	3	4	5	19	25	10
Bristol Rovers	12	5	4	5	18	28	10
Queen's Park Rangers ...	11	4	1	6	20	21	9
Clapton Orient ...	11	3	3	5	17	25	9
Luton Town	12	3	3	6	16	17	9
Walsall	11	3	1	7	23	30	7
Norwich City	11	1	4	6	10	25	6
Newport County ...	11	2	1	8	13	29	5
Thames	11	2	1	8	13	29	5

League Goal Scorers.		
FOWLER	...	9
TRICKER	...	3
FLETCHER	...	1
GALBRAITH	...	1
VANNER	...	1
EDMONDS	...	1
SANDERS	...	1

City's team for the game at Clapton Orient was the backbone for the stirring cup games around the corner.

The Cup run started at Northfleet United with a 3-0 win. Then Coventry City were beaten 2-1 in a replay on their own ground after a 1-1 tie at St James's Park before the draw for the Third Round gave City the plum tie – a home game with First Division giants Derby County. Exeter won 3-2 in front of 16,500 fans after George Jobey, the Rams' manager who had watched Exeter play two weeks before the game, was reputed to have said 'My "A" team could beat them'. City then travelled to meet well-placed Division Two side Bury. Here is the team at St David's station on their way to Gigg Lane. From left to right, back row: Billy McDevitt (Manager), Reg Clarke, George Purcell, Ted Jones (Trainer), Charlie Miller, Bob Shanks, Arthur Doncaster, Mr McGahey (Chairman), Richard Baugh, Arthur Davies, Harold `Happy' Houghton, Stan Barber, Billy Armfield, Jock Angus, Percy Varco, Mr S.H. Thomas (Director), Mr W. Lake (Director).

Exeter won the cup-tie at Bury 2-1. Their hero in that game was 'keeper Arthur Davies, who is seen here punching clear in a *Western Weekly News* photograph during some goalmouth pressure.

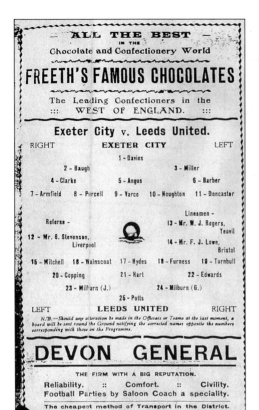

Exeter City v. Leeds United.

RIGHT   **EXETER CITY**   LEFT

1 – Davies

2 – Baugh   3 – Miller

4 – Clarke   5 – Angus   6 – Barber

7 – Armfield   8 – Purcell   9 – Yarco   10 – Houghton   11 – Doncaster

Linesmen –

Referee –   13 – Mr. W. J. Rogers, Yeovil

12 – Mr. B. Stevenson, Liverpool   14 – Mr. F. J. Lowe, Bristol

15 – Mitchell   16 – Wainscoat   17 – Hydes   18 – Furness   19 – Turnbull

20 – Copping   21 – Hart   22 – Edwards

23 – Milburn (J.)   24 – Milburn (G.)

25 – Potts

LEFT   **LEEDS UNITED**   RIGHT

N.B.—Should any alteration be made in the Officials or Teams at the last moment, a board will be sent round the Ground notifying the corrected names opposite the numbers corresponding with those on the Programmes.

City beat Leeds 3-1 in the Fifth Round at St James's Park, Billy Armfield (2) and George Purcell scoring in front of 19,130 people. It was the Yorkshire club's second visit to Exeter – two years earlier, in the Third Round in 1928/28, they had drawn 2-2 and gone back to Elland Road for a comfortable 5-1 win. The City line-up was that given in the programme.

Leeds 'keeper, Petts, in action at St James's Park. He was to have a good game but was beaten three times as Exeter went through to the Sixth Round for the first time in their history.

The Sixth Round and an 800 mile trip to Roker Park to meet Sunderland, the 'team of all talents'. The *Express & Echo* football edition's cartoon shows a City player heading north with 'bags of confidence'. What the 'best oysters' are for is not certain. The mascot on the car represents Dido, the seagull who was said to ensure a City win if he perched on the crossbar during a game. Grateful fans even brought fish to reward him. After asking how you tell one seagull from another, the more cynical of us (perhaps the more sensible) would say that the best way to attract seagulls is indeed to feed them – but why spoil a legend? Later versions of Dido are said to have existed, including stuffed ones. The reasoning behind the bird's name is unclear, but there are several possibilities: the most likely being that he was named after the groundsman (who was also nicknamed Dido).

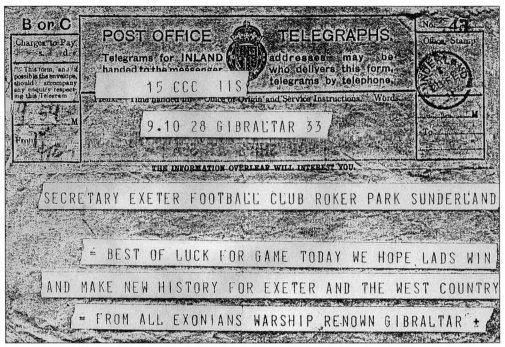

SECRETARY EXETER FOOTBALL CLUB ROKER PARK SUNDERLAND

= BEST OF LUCK FOR GAME TODAY WE HOPE LADS WIN

AND MAKE NEW HISTORY FOR EXETER AND THE WEST COUNTRY

= FROM ALL EXONIANS WARSHIP RENOWN GIBRALTAR +

Waiting at Roker Park for Exeter City was a mountain of 'Good Luck' telegrams from all over the world, especially from Devonians. This included the Exeter men serving with the Royal Navy on *HMS Warspite* at Gibraltar (above). City's opponents in the 'bread-and-butter' League games were behind them as well, this telegram from Brighton & Hove Albion (below) being typical of support for them throughout the Third Division.

THOMAS EXETER CITY FOOTBALL CLUB ROKER PARK GROUND

SUNDERLAND

GOOD LUCK BRIGHTON AND HOVE ALBION +++

Harold Houghton's goal brought City a 1-1 draw at Roker Park and the chance to bring Sunderland back to Exeter. They would be the third Division One side to visit the city that season – surely a record for the Third Division – and attracted the club's record gate when 20,984 people paid to get into St James's Park on Wednesday 4 March 1931. In the first match, Exeter had played before 51,642 people at Roker Park, easily the biggest crowd ever to watch them. There were several thousand fans, not forgetting the Exeter City Band, waiting at St David's Station when the City party returned from Sunderland. Such was their greetings that the match programme notes for the replay thanked the supporters for the 'hearty reception given the players on their return' and went on to hope 'they can do an equal service this afternoon by good, strong, vocal support'.

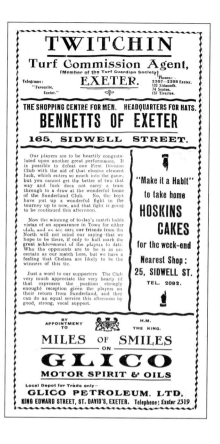

Once again City were able to field the team printed in the programme.

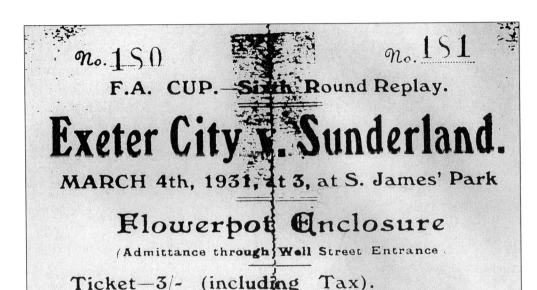

no. 150   no. 151

F.A. CUP.—Sixth Round Replay.

Exeter City v. Sunderland.

MARCH 4th, 1931, at 3, at S. James' Park

Flowerpot Enclosure

(Admittance through Well Street Entrance.

Ticket—3/- (including Tax).

Not many tickets for the Sunderland replay survive. At the time they were worth their weight in gold and, when they went on sale, the fans queued for hours to get their hands on one.

All good things come to an end. City ended the 1930/31 campaign with a 2-0 win at home to Queen's Park Rangers – but was it a good season? There can be no doubt the answer is yes, even if League form went begging at times and the club's final position in the Division Three (South) table was a lowly thirteenth. The *Express & Echo* said it all with this end-of-season cartoon.

After finishing seventh in 1931/32, the following season Exeter City went as close to Division Two as they ever would when they finished as runners-up to Brentford in Division Three (South). In the end they were four points behind the London club, due in no small way to the fact that they only picked up ten points from their first nine games. They won seventeen and drew six of the next twenty-five but dropped points in the closing games of the season. Exeter lost 2-1 at home to Brentford but exacted a 2-0 revenge when they went to Griffin Park later in the campaign. During that fine mid-season run, Devon rivals Torquay United were beaten 5-0 at St James's Park on 28 January 1933. Maybe City skipper Charlie Miller (right) knew something as he is wearing a broad smile as he tosses up before the game.

How the *Express & Echo* football cartoonist, Jos Walker, saw the City players of the early 1930s.

The strong man of Exeter City's famous cup run – and indeed, throughout his ten years with the club – was Exeter-born Reg Clarke. Universally known as 'Nobby' he played in the same Ladysmith Road School team as Cliff Bastin. The two made their City debuts towards the end of the 1927/28 season: Reg's was at Newport on 22 March 1928, when Exeter lost 1-0. In all he was to play 338 League and cup games for the club, including all the 1930/31 cup ties and all forty-two matches in the 1932/33 runners-up season. Throughout his time at Exeter he attracted many accolades from the press, who saw him as a 'hard-working right-half' who 'has never let his side down' and was 'one of the soundest wing half-backs in the South'. His memorable connections with Exeter were severed in 1937 when he became the landlord of the Volunteer Inn at Ottery St Mary. Exeter City had a rule that stated that no one, while a registered player with the club, should take over a licensed house. Although he was prepared to play for City at a reduced wage, he was put on the transfer list and, despite interest from Wrexham and Barrow, moved on a free transfer to Aldershot and played for the Hampshire club until just after the Second World War.

Reg Clarke leads out Exeter City at St James's Park to meet Leicester City for his benefit match in September 1933. Harold Webb and Jack Angus are directly behind him. Reg used the money from the game to buy a house in Seaton: he had married a Seaton girl, later became the licensee of the Kings Arms at Seaton and, for about a dozen years, was treasurer to Seaton Town AFC. His last game of football was when he was nearing his fiftieth birthday and turned out for Seaton's 'Over 30s' side against the 'Under 30s'. The younger men won 3-0.

The six new men for the final practice match at the start of the 1934/35 season were, from left to right, back row: John Dryden, Joe McClure, Dudley Lewis. Front row: Cornelius Tierney, Sam Dudley, Edward McArthur. None of them stayed long at St James's Park.

Exeter City line-up from the early 1930s. From left to right, back row: Billy McDevitt (Manager), Reg Clarke, Richard Baugh, Arthur Davies, Charlie Miller, Stan Barber. Front row: Billy Armfield, George Purcell, Percy Varco, Harold Houghton, Arthur Doncaster, Jock Angus.

EXETER'S CUP-FIGHTERS CARICATURED BY "MATT"

CHAS. MILLER

LESLIE DENNINGTON
(Left Half)

VARCO
(CENTRE FORWARD)

STANLEY BARBER
(LEFT HALF)

JOHN ANGUS
(CENTRE HALF)

W. ARMFIELD
(OUTSIDE RIGHT)

REG CLARKE (RIGHT HALF)

GEORGE PURCELL
(INSIDE RIGHT)

ROBERT SHANKS
(LEFT FULL BACK)

DONCASTER
(OUTSIDE LEFT)

HAROLD HOUGHTON
(INSIDE LEFT)

RICHARD BAUGH
(RIGHT BACK)

TELESCOPIC STUDY
OF ARTHUR DAVIES
(GOALKEEPER)

A TRAINER
IN TRAINING
(MR TED JONES)

MR McDEVITT (MANAGER)

This week "Matt," the *Sunday Graphic* caricaturist, presents members and officials of the Exeter City F.C. How well he has "caught" them it is for you to say. Exeter City will welcome Leeds United next Saturday.

Just how much Exeter City's cup exploits caught the eye of the nation can, perhaps, best be gauged from their being caricatured in the *Sunday Graphic* by its famous caricaturist `Matt'.

'If it is not hurting it is not doing any good'. If this is indeed the case then, judging by the smiles as the City men get down to training in readiness for the 1934/35 season, this run is not doing them any good at all.

Exeter City have had more than their fair share of being on the wrong end of giant-killing acts in the FA Cup. The first occasion was in the 1922/23 season when Bath City won 2-1 at St James's Park. In 1934/35 City, having beating fellow Division Three (South) side Charlton Athletic 5-2 at home in a replay, travelled to Southern League Yeovil Town and their famous (or should that be infamous?) sloping Huish pitch. Again, maybe City skipper Charlie Miller (right) knew something as he greets Yeovil captain Louis Page before the game. He doesn't look too happy and, sure enough, Yeovil won 4-1.

This picture must have been taken between 1932 and 1936. It is probably of Henry Poulter scoring a goal against Corinthians. Poulter, who came from Sunderland as an amateur, was unable to get a regular place in the side and played only fifty League games for the club. This is somewhat surprising, considering the fact that he scored thirty-three goals, mostly at inside or centre forward. This must have been a friendly game, as there is no record of Exeter meeting Corinthians in any competitive fixture around this time.

Exeter City, 1936/37 season.

The crush barriers being strengthened at the Popular End during the 1930s. Of special interest in this picture is the small press box at the side of the grandstand and the rather untidy area, to its right, where the club's offices now stand.

Goalmouth action at St James's Park in the mid-1930s, with Clapton Orient keeper W.Robertson going up for a high ball. Orient did not change their name to Leyton Orient until the end of the Second World War.

Below: In the 1933/34 season, Exeter City became the first winners of the Division Three (South) KO Cup, beating Devon neighbours Torquay United 1-0 in the final at Home Park, in front of 6,000 people. Stan Hurst scored the all-important goal. In the First Round, City beat Crystal Palace 11-6 at St James's Park with six of the goals coming from Fred Whitlow. They went on to defeat Coventry City 1-0 away (after a 1-1 draw at home) and then needed three Semi-final clashes with Brighton & Hove Albion to decide who went through. The first game at Craven Cottage, Fulham, ended as a 1-1 draw, the first replay (at St James's Park) also ended 1-1 following extra time: this picture shows Exeter attacking the Brighton goal during this game. The second replay was at Brighton, where Exeter won 4-3.

DIVISION III (SOUTH)							
	P	W	D	L	F	A	Pts.
Coventry C.	42	24	9	9	102	45	57
Luton T.	42	22	12	8	81	45	56
Reading	42	26	2	14	87	62	54
Q.P.R.	42	22	9	11	84	53	53
Watford	42	20	9	13	80	54	49
C. Palace	42	22	5	15	96	74	49
Brighton	42	18	8	16	70	63	44
Bournemouth	42	16	11	15	60	56	43
Notts Co.	42	15	12	15	60	57	42
Torquay U.	42	16	9	17	62	62	41
Aldershot	42	14	12	16	53	61	40
Millwall	42	14	12	16	58	71	40
Bristol C.	42	15	10	17	48	59	40
Clapton O.	42	16	6	20	55	61	38
Northampton	42	15	8	19	62	90	38
Gillingham	42	14	9	19	66	77	37
Bristol R.	42	14	9	19	69	95	37
Southend U.	42	13	10	19	61	62	36
Swindon T.	42	14	8	20	64	73	36
Cardiff C.	42	13	10	19	60	73	36
Newport Co.	42	11	9	22	60	111	31
Exeter C.	42	8	11	23	59	93	27

Although City slowly slid down the Division Three (South) table between 1932/33 and 1934/35 – finishing second, ninth and eleventh – being bottom at the end of the 1935/36 season and having to apply for re-election came as a great shock to all at the club. The great cup team was breaking up and manager Billy McDevitt left at the end of September 1935 when Exeter, after winning 5-1 at home to Aldershot on the opening day of the season, picked up only one point from their next eight games. There was a run in November and December when thirteen of the fourteen points on offer were taken, but after that only one of the last twenty-one games brought a win.

Maybe training was not as hard for the professional footballer in the 1930s as it is today (of course the cynic might add that the modern player gets a lot more money). However, it was still treated as a important part of a player's life as the serious looks on these squad members' faces suggest.

One of the casualties in the clear out at the end of the 1935/36 season was Jimmy Gray. He played 221 games for City, almost always at right-back, in the seven seasons following 1929/30, when he had joined Exeter from Liverpool. His former club visited St James's Park for Gray's benefit match on 1 May 1935, when 5,000 people saw Liverpool win 3-1. The officials and players are, from left to right: A. Martin (Referee), Dick Pym (Linesman). Exeter City: Davies, Gray, Miller, Angus, Webb, Lewis, J. Scott, T. Scott, Hurst, McArthur, Dryden. Liverpool: Kane, Cooper, Tennant, Savage, McDougall, Dobbs, Niewenhuys, Wright, English, Johnson, Hanson.

The City squad report to St James's Park in July 1936 for training. From left to right, back row: Pollard, Hobbs, Stimpson, Bamsey, Tierney, Young, Scott. Middle row: Shadwell, Brown, Boyle, Angus, Chesters, Clarke, Lowton (Assistant Trainer). Front row: Ormon, McGill, Johnson, Williams, Kerr, Ebdon, Smith.

The Exeter City Football and Athletic Co., Ltd.

Members of the Football Association,
the Football League Third Division
and Southern.

Chairman:
Mr. M. J. McGAHEY

Secretary:
Mr. S. H. THOMAS

Players' Manager:
Mr. JACK ENGLISH

ST. JAMES' PARK,
EXETER.

4th May, 1936.

Dear Sir,

My Club is compelled to apply for re-election to the Southern Section, and it is a matter of great regret to us that we are in the position of having to do so.

Exeter City became a professional Club in the year 1908 joining the old Southern League, and from that day to this we have carried out every obligation, both to the Leagues we are Members of, and to the Clubs we are associated with.

Five years ago we went into the draw for the Semi-Final of the F.A. Cup in company with Sunderland, upon whose ground we drew, only, however, to be defeated in the replay at Exeter, and we were fortunate enough to defeat that Season in the Competition, Coventry City at Coventry, Bury at Bury, Leeds United at Exeter, and Derby County at Exeter.

The next Season we fought out the Championship of the Section with Brentford finishing Second to that Club in the League Table.

From that year we have spent considerable sums of money in transfer fees in the hope that promotion might be achieved, and during the past unsuccessful Season paid nearly £1,500 in players' transfers with that object,

Ack/ May 14th/ JyG

Finishing in the two bottom places in either sections of the Third Division meant that the unfortunate clubs concerned had to seek re-election, thus competing with non-league clubs that had aspirations to better themselves. Usually, although not a cast-iron certainty, the clubs going cap-in-hand to their fellow members received the benefit of the 'old pals' act. Finishing

not an inconsiderable sum for a Third Division Club. The lesson we have learnt is that money is not a certain road to success in football.

One of the reasons for our non-success has been injuries to players. On the opening match of the Season we lost the services of our First Team centre forward and he has remained unfit to play, and bad luck in this direction has dogged us right through the year.

Exeter with a population of 70,000 is the Capital of the County, with an immediate surrounding population of a much larger number, and with reasonable success we are always able to command gates sufficient to run a good team.

During the Cup year referred to we took the following gates at Exeter:

	£	s.	d.
Derby County	1,669	0	0
Leeds United	2,397	0	0
Sunderland (Mid-Week Replay) ...	2,558	0	0

and in League Matches with Plymouth Argyle, when they were in the Third Division, we have taken gates exceeding £1,000.

With regard to players we shall, of course, place two professional sides in the field, in the Third Division and Southern League, most of these players have already been signed on for next season.

FINANCIALLY we are in a wonderful position for a Third Division Club.

We have no bank overdraft, our directors, therefore, have no need to give any guarantee to the Bank.

The Club owns its own ground valued at £20,000 subject to a mortgage of £8,000 only.

It is sheer misfortune that compels us to seek your assistance and we feel certain that we shall not ask in vain. The Capital City of the West cannot do without its League Football.

Thanking you in anticipation,

Yours faithfully,

Chairman.

bottom in 1935/36 meant that Exeter City had to re-apply and, as was the custom, they wrote to all the clubs who would be voting on their fate, extolling the virtues of having them in Division Three (South). They were successful, as indeed they would be twelve months later when – finishing one off the bottom – they had to apply again.

Charlie Miller was probably the best skipper ever to lead Exeter City and was in charge during the great FA Cup campaign of 1930/31 and the runners-up season of 1932/33. A Scot, he came to St James's Park from Plymouth Argyle (where he had few chances to shine) in 1926 and inherited the captaincy from Les Dennington at the start of the 1930/31 season. By the time he retired and took over a local pub in 1936, he had played 297 games for City, mostly as a left-back.

Goalmouth drama at St James's Park in the 1930s. Emery, a Newport County forward (out of sight) has tried his luck with a shot.

Although they had to apply for re-election in 1936/37 after finishing next to bottom, City had another good cup run that season, reaching the Fifth Round – where they lost 5-3 to Preston North End at Deepdale. In the earlier rounds, they beat Folkstone (3-0), Walthamstow Avenue (3-2), Oldham Athletic (3-0) and Leicester City (3-1). The picture shows Jack Angus shaking hands with the driver before the Exeter party leave St David's station for the game at Preston.

During the 1930s, a 'Former City XI' played the current team at St James's Park with much interest being shown in the presence of Dick Pym as goalkeeper. The team was, from left to right, back row: Reg Loram, Miller, -?-, Crawshaw, Potter, McDevitt, -?-. Front row: Newman, Armfield, Pym, -?-, Ditchburn, -?-.

Arthur Davies, the City goalkeeper, in action here for the City Reserves against Plymouth Argyle Reserves at Home Park in a Southern League game around 1935. He is being challenged by Argyle forwards Clarke and Simpson. Davies had two seasons with Everton before coming to Exeter, for whom he made 177 appearances between 1930 and 1935 – including a run of 124 consecutive games. Injury cost him his place to Arthur Chesters and he joined Plymouth Argyle.

The practice game at the start of the 1937/38 season has attracted a fair sized crowd to St James's Park to watch the Stripes play the Whites. In this goalmouth incident, the ball appears to have cleared the bar but, in the surprising absence of goal nets, one cannot be certain. The cross bar, just a plank of wood, may not meet with modern referees' approval either.

Jack Angus, despite his name, was a Geordie and not a Scot. He joined Exeter City from Scunthorpe as a centre half in time to play at Bury in the 1930/31 Cup run. He would stay with the club until 1947/48, when he retired as a professional footballer after 265 appearances in a City shirt.

The season that never was. Most English League sides had played three or four games of the 1939/40 season when the Second World War broke out and, for reasons that are not particularly sound, these games never counted towards a players' appearances or goal totals. City's squad for the season lines up for the official picture. From left to right, back row: Windle, Steve Walker, Vincent Blore, Charlie Thomson, Stan Cutting. Middle row: Freeman, Hartill, Leach, Jack Angus, Henry Bowl, Jack Blood, Charlie Sutherley, Smith, Cyril Crawshaw. Front row: Jimmy Gallagher, Harold Riley, John Shadwell, Dick Ebdon, Bill Fellowes, John Little, George Wardle.

Three

A Fresh Start

City have played many friendly games with local amateur teams, often raising much-needed funds for them. Here, however, The Grecians have turned out at Bradninch against the local cricket club in the summer of 1947, at the end of the first post-war soccer season. Arthur Coles is fifth from the right in the front row, whilst Glyn Vaughan is two places away from him to his right. Dick Pym is on the extreme left of the back row.

DIVISION III (SOUTH)

	P	W	D	L	F	A	Pts.
Cardiff C.	42	30	6	6	93	30	66
Q.P.R.	42	23	11	8	74	40	57
Bristol C.	42	20	11	11	94	56	51
Swindon T.	42	19	11	12	84	73	49
Walsall	42	17	12	13	74	59	46
Ipswich T.	42	16	14	12	61	53	46
Bournemouth	42	18	8	16	72	54	44
Southend U.	42	17	10	15	71	60	44
Reading	42	16	11	15	83	74	43
Port Vale	42	17	9	16	68	63	43
Torquay U.	42	15	12	15	52	61	42
Notts Co.	42	15	10	17	63	63	40
Northampton	42	15	10	17	72	75	40
Bristol R.	42	16	8	18	59	69	40
Exeter C.	42	15	9	18	60	69	39
Watford	42	17	5	20	61	76	39
Brighton	42	13	12	17	54	72	38
C. Palace	42	13	11	18	49	62	37
Leyton O.	42	12	8	22	54	75	32
Aldershot	42	10	12	20	48	78	32
Norwich C.	42	10	8	24	64	100	28
Mansfield T.	42	9	10	23	48	96	28

St James's Park was requisitioned by the War Department soon after the outbreak of the Second World War and was later used by the US army for training and camping purposes. It is said that such was the state of the ground after the war that it was touch-and-go whether the club could carry on. It did, playing some Regional (Division Three – South of the Thames) football in 1945/46 and then entertained Torquay United on August 31 1946 in the opening Division Three (South) game when the English League resumed for the 1946/47 season. Ray Wright scored City's goal in a 1-1 draw. More importantly, to a club that was not in the best of financial circumstances at the time, there were 11,468 people at the game and gates were to remain healthy, even though only one win in the their last ten games saw City finish well down the table.

Three Exeter City players just after the war were, from left to right: Ray Wright, George Wardle and Bert Hammond. Wardle left for Cardiff City in 1947. Wright, who joined City from Wolverhampton Wanderers, departed a year later, joining Yeovil Town.

Single sheet programmes for Reserve team and practice matches were the order of the day in the immediate post-war years, when paper was rationed. Such programmes are collectors' pieces today, fetching as much as ten pounds – 2,400 times its original cover value of a penny on 16 August 1947 when the 'Colours' played the 'Whites' in the final practice game. The sides were obviously picked for a good match. Seven days later, when City lost 4-0 at Walsall in their opening league game of the season, the forward line was the same that played here for the 'Whites', whilst the goalkeeper and defence were all 'Colours'.

EXETER CITY F. & A. Co., Ltd.

OFFICIAL PROGRAMME 1d.

FINAL PRACTICE MATCH

COLOURS *versus* WHITES

SATURDAY, AUGUST 16th, 1947

Kick-off 3.15 p.m.

Right	COLOURS	Left
	HOYLE	
THOMPSON (2)		BLOOD (3)
CUTTING (4)	BARTHOLOMEW (5)	WALKER (6)
SUTHERLAND (8)		VAUGHAN (10)
GRANVILLE (7)	SMART (9)	FALLON, W. (11)

Referee : Mr. R. JEWELL

Linesmen :
Mr. M. McNAMARA (Red Flag)
Mr. W. TAYLOR (Blue Flag)

REGAN (11)	EBDON (9)	HUTCHINGS (7)
	WRIGHT (10)	EVANS (8)
COLES (6)	DAVEY (5)	GIBSON (4)
JOHNSTONE (3)		D. WARREN (2)
	SINGLETON	
Left	WHITES	Right

SATURDAY NEXT, AUGUST 23rd, 1947

Kick-off 3.15 p.m.

LOVELL'S ATHLETIC

SOUTHERN LEAGUE

Action from the 'Colours' against the 'Whites' practice game.

Exeter City may not have cut too much ice in the immediate post-war years but Mrs Louisa 'Amy' Farrow of Exeter had her memories to keep her warm. She had the autographs of the 1930/31 FA Cup run team (she was Miss Louisa Anstead in those days) and proudly shows them off here.

The ball hits the Grecian's crossbar during a Norwich City attack in the 1947/48 season at St James's Park. City won 2-0 courtesy of an own goal and one from Duggie Regan.

Two players run out for a 1940s game at St James's Park. One of them obviously means business, judging by the way he is rolling up his sleeves. The baggy shorts will bring back memories to an older generation of supporters.

Action in the City goalmouth at St James's Park in the 1940s.

EXETER CITY FOOTBALL CLUB
Official Programme

PRICE 3d

Vol. 5   No. 9
EXETER CITY
versus
WATFORD
Third Division
SATURDAY, 6th NOVEMBER, 1948

Exeter City programmes in the years following the Second World War showed the not-unattractive, red-and-white hooped shirts, which the Grecians wore until 1950 when they changed to all red. This footballer was a bit of a cult figure on programmes of the day. He could be found in black and white on Torquay's programmes and also appeared on at least those of Colchester and Ipswich.

Exeter City versus Watford on 6 November 1948. A crowd of 7,739 people watched Exeter win 2-1, with goals by Angus Mackay and Bill Dymond. It was Derek Warren's home debut – he had played for the first time the previous Saturday at the Vetch Field in front of 29,000 people who saw Swansea, the league leaders, trounce City 6-0. Warren came from Colyton and played for Yeovil Town, Taunton Town and Seaton Town after he left Exeter in 1952

Join the Territorial Army in Exeter & District

EXETER CITY
Colours—Red and White Hoops

Right   Left
HOYLE
1
WARREN   CLARK
2   3
FALLON   DAVEY   WALKER
4   5   6
DYMOND   EVANS   JOHNSTON   MACKAY   REGAN
7   8   9   10   11

Referee: Linesmen:
Mr. C. J. WAKLEY   Mr. W. E. Keel (Red Stripe)
(Somerton)   Mr. R. L. Buscombe (Blue Stripe)

CUMNER   DRURY   THOMAS   OSBORNE   DAVIES, W.
11   10   9   8   7
PATON   RATCLIFFE   EGGLESTON
6   5   4
OLLIVER   HARRIS
3   2
DAVIES
1
WATFORD
(Blue and White)

Left   Right

Infantry—4th Bn. The Devonshire Regt. T.A.

Sport, Comradeship & Pay for Training

Hut 5, HIGHER BARRACKS, Exeter

The Grecians Association was formed in 1945 and made a considerable contribution to the finances of the parent club, handing over some £25,000 in the first twenty years of its existence and paying for the Grecian Gate to be built. It merged with the Exeter City Supporters' Club in 1970, the two bodies becoming the Exeter City Supporters' Club (the Grecians). How Exeter City became known as The Grecians is shrouded in the mists of time. The most popular theory is that it came about because the people of St Sidwell's – a parish of which St James's Park was once a part of – were known as 'Greeks'. One pre-war City favourite, Reg Clarke, bought a house in Eyewell Green, Seaton, with his benefit money and called it 'Grecian'. It still bears this name today, over sixty years later.

OGDEN'S CIGARETTES

EXETER CITY

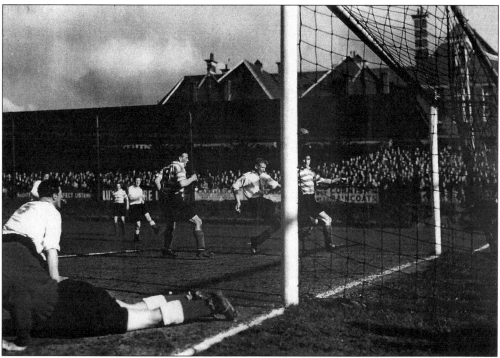

Exeter City's goal under pressure at St James's Park, around 1948.

Fred Davey was a very popular half-back who made his debut for The Grecians against Bristol City at St James's Park on Boxing Day, 1947. In a career that spanned from 1947 until 1956 he played in 295 League and cup games for Exeter and was regarded as the epitome of a sportsman by all who knew him. Given a free transfer at the end of his time at Exeter, he joined Bridgwater Town and then played for his native Crediton in the Exeter & District League for a few seasons.

With City now wearing their all-red strip, this picture of a game at St James's Park has to be from the early 1950s.

Exeter City's first post-war manager, George Roughton, arrived at St James's Park in October 1945 with impeccable First Division references, having made 250 appearances for Huddersfield Town and Manchester United before the war. He did play a few games for Exeter in regional football in 1945/46 but then ended his playing days. Like so many City managers, a lack of cash prevented him from attaining much managerial success but he was a popular and much-respected man. Rumour linked him with the manager's job at Liverpool but he eventually went to Southampton in 1952.

City press at home, around 1952.

Like Fred Davey (see p. 58), Keith Harvey was a Kyrtonian (a Crediton man to the non-Devonian) and the two often played in the same defence between the 1952/53 season and the 1955/56 season – when Davey left the club. He was an outstanding centre half in his career, which spanned from 1952 until 1969. In that time, he played no less than 483 League games in City colours. He is always cited as having played in less League games than City's record holder, Arnold Mitchell (see p. 61), who made 495 appearances. But if, as you must, you add the two players' cup games to those totals, Fred Davey played for Exeter 517 times – one more than Mitchell.

The 1956/57 playing staff line up before a practice match at St James's Park. From left to right, back row: John Porteous, Keith Harvey, Steve Parr, Frank Houghton, John Lobbett, George Hunter, George Ferrier, Marsh, Norman Packer. Middle row: Bowkett, Alan Sword, Jim Currie, Colin Beer, Eric Phoenix, Dennis Simpson, Raymond John. Front row: Graham Rees, Brian Doyle, Dave Robinson, Ron Burke, Arnold Mitchell, Theo Foley, John Divers, George Willis, Edward Buckle.

Arnold Mitchell was a much-travelled man when he came to Exeter City in July 1952, having seen service with Sheffield Wednesday, Derby County, Nottingham Forest and Notts County. He stayed with The Grecians until the 1965/66 season, when he retired. He then played a few games for Taunton Town. For Exeter City he was played mainly as an inside forward but did, in fact, turn out for the club in all eleven positions – including goalkeeper when the regular man was injured during a game. In all he played 516 League and cup games for Exeter, one less than Fred Davey (see p. 60).

Glyn Vaughan, Arthur Coles and Jack Blood in 'civvies' at St James's Park. Coles was yet another Crediton man to play for City, joining them in 1936 and, after playing in Northern Ireland, coming back for a second spell in 1939. When he finally left the club, in 1946, he joined Barnstaple Town.

Barney Singleton, with Jim Murray in close attendance, collects a high ball at St James's Park, around 1949. Singleton came to Exeter from Wolverhampton Wanderers in 1946 and played for The Grecians until 1954, when he retired after being given a free transfer. He died in 1981 aged only fifty-seven.

Steve Challis, Bert Hoyle and 'Digger' Ebdon helping to build the turnstile for the 'Jungle' Gate at the side of the grandstand. It got its name from the considerable number of brambles that had to be removed to get near enough to start work.

The 1948/49 playing staff at St James's Park. From left to right, back row: Jim Clark, Stan Rowe, Ken Powell, Cyril Johnstone, Reg Gibson, Archie Smith, Steve Walker, Bill Dymond. Middle row: Ron Johnston, Harry Bartholomew, Arthur Coles, Bert Hoyle, Barney Singleton, Derek Warren, Bob Jeffrey, Fred Davey. Front row: Jimmy Gallagher (Trainer), Duggie Regan, Peter Fallon, Bill Rowe, Harry Evans, Bill Fellowes (Assistant Secretary), George Roughton (Manager), Angus Mackay, Bernard Grant, Dennis Hutchings, Dick Smart, Stan Cutting (Assistant Trainer).

City attending an away game, c. 1949. From left to right, back row: -?-, Jim Gallaher, George Roughton (Manager), Jim Clark, Bert Hoyle, Bill Harrower, Steve Walker, -?-. Front row: Mr Rigby (Director), Bill Dymond, Archie Smith, Dick Smart, Angus Mackay, Peter Fallon, Johnson.

After beating non-league Barnet and Hereford United, Exeter City were drawn away to Division Two side Grimsby Town in the Third Round of the FA Cup in 1948/49: they lost 2-1. Training here in Grimsby, before the game, are: Bill Dymond, Archie Smith. Bill Harrower and Jim Clark.

Bert Hoyle saves at St James's Park around 1950, shortly before he left the club for Bristol Rovers. The other city defenders are, from left to right: Steve Walker, Peter Fallon and Derek Warren.

Barney Singleton comes across to make a save in a practice match, *c.* 1951. Derek Warren is in the white shirt.

Barney Singleton played 189 League and cup games for City between 1946 and 1954 before his testimonial game against Swansea Town. The referee of that match, Mr Ellis, is on the left and Duggie Regan is on the right-hand side of the picture. On Barney's immediate left is the secretary, Sidney Thomas, whose father, Sidney Thomas (senior), was the club's first secretary in 1904 and served it for the best part of seventy years – latterly as a director, chairman and then president.

EXETER CITY FOOTBALL CLUB
Official Programme

PRICE 3^d

Vol. 7 No. 15

EXETER CITY
VERSUS
CHELSEA
F.A. Cup—4th Round

Chelsea provided St James's Park regulars with their first view of Division One opposition for some years when they drew 1-1 in a FA Cup Fourth Round game at Exeter on 27 January 1951. There were 20,000 at the game, in which City right-back Derek Warren was outstanding and attracted the attention of the London side's manager.

The City line-up given in the programme was the team that played in the game. For a habitually cash-strapped club like Exeter City, the gate receipts of £3,760 were a godsend. They took a third (£1,250) and later received a share of the Cup Pool – a third of all gate receipts from the Third, Fourth, Fifth and Sixth Round games and a quarter from the semi-finals.

City's Ray Goddard (right), a former Chelsea favourite, goes up for the ball with Bobby Smith. Goalkeeper Barney Singleton is almost obscured behind them. Also present are Roy Bentley and City defenders, Jim Clark and Bill Harrower.

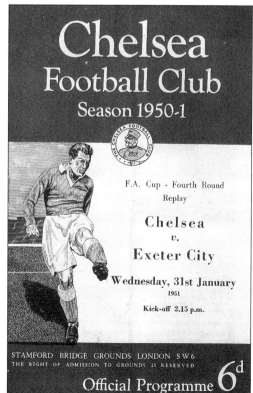

There were 40,000 people there to see Exeter City lose the replay 2-0. Seventeen-year-old Bobby Smith, later to make his name with Spurs and England, scored both goals from rebounds off the woodwork.

Exeter City Players

WARREN

SINGLETON

CLARK

HARROWER

DOYLE

DAVEY

McCLELLAND

SMITH

REGAN

LYNN

FALLON

CHELSEA

Colours—Shirts: Blue (White Collars). Knickers: White. Stockings: Black, Blue and White Tops.

(Goal)
Pickering

2. (Right-back)
Bathgate

3. (Left-back)
Hughes

4. (Right-half)
Armstrong

5. (Centre-half)
Harris
(Captain)

6. (Left-half)
Dickson

7. (Outside-right)
Gray

8. (Inside-right)
Campbell

9. (Centre-forward)
Smith (R.)

10. (Inside-left)
Bentley

11. (Outside-left)
Williams

Referee:
Mr. R. C. CARTER
(Swindon)

Linesmen:
Mr. B. C. CROSS (Clacton)
(Red Flag)

Mr. A. G. COOK (Chichester)
(Yellow Flag)

(Extra time will be played if necessary)

Regan   **Lynn**   **Smith**   **Fallon**   **McClelland**

11. (Outside-left)   10. (Inside-left)   9. (Centre-forward)   8. (Inside-right)   7. (Outside-right)

Davey   **Goddard**   **Harrower**

6. (Left-half)   5. (Centre-half)   4. (Right-half)

Clark   **Warren**

3. (Left-back)   2. (Right-back)

Singleton
(Goal)

EXETER CITY

Colours—Shirts: Red, White Collars   Knickers: White, Stockings: Red and White.

After the end of the 1950/51 season, Exeter City made a four-game tour of the Netherlands, meeting DOS Utrecht (won 3-0), Haarlem's Elftal (won 5-3), Hertogenbosch (lost 2-4) and a Combined Hague XI (won 2-0). The win against Haarlem was particularly impressive as the Dutch side had no less than seven internationals in their line-up. Above: the two teams pose before the match at Harlem. Below: the City party pays a visit to the tulip fields.

Surely few City programme collectors will have this one this in their collection. Nor would many City fans relish the prospect of having to shout 'Get your glasses on Scheidsrechter' when the referee misses an obvious (to the fan) handball.

The friendly with local Exeter & District League club Crediton United in 1956 was a relatively unimportant game in the history of Exeter City. However, this is one of very few team pictures with Maurice Setters in it. A Honitonian, Setters only played eleven games for Exeter City, in the 1954/55 season, before going on to better things as a player with West Bromwich Albion, Manchester United – where he collected the FA Cup at Wembley as the club's captain – Stoke City, Coventry City and Charlton Athletic. Exeter City are, from left to right, back row: Arnold Mitchell, Fred Davey, Charlie McClelland, Dick Walton, Keith Harvey, Norman Douglas. Front row: Gerry Priestley, John Anderson, Angus Mackay, Bill Ellaway, Maurice Setters. For Davey and Harvey, of course, this was a trip home.

71

Attendances remained good (by today's standards) throughout the 1940s and 1950s. Above: a crowd of 8,162 watched City beat Swindon 3-1 with goals from Angus Mackay (2) and Gerald Priestley in a midweek match at St James Park. A lot of them seem to have chosen the Popular End to watch the game from. Below: at the start of the 1955/56 season, the Popular End again lived up to its name when 13,991 fans crowed into St James's Park to watch a goal-less draw with Torquay United. Trust the ladies to get the best places when there is a photographer around!

Four

The Swinging Sixties
and Seventies

If the Sixties swung for Exeter City it would have been in the 1963/64 when the side finished fourth in the Fourth Division and were promoted to Division Three. Exeter had finished bottom in Division Three (South) in 1957/58 and become founder members of the new Division Four the following season. In 1963/64 they needed a point from their last game at Workington to make sure they went up. A goal-less draw brought promotion. Here, skipper Arnold Mitchell signs autographs for the fans on the team's return. Des Anderson is to his right and Alan Banks is on the right-hand side of the picture. One optimistic supporter holds aloft a banner saying 'Grand Show Exeter Now Div 2'. Maybe one day!

When Exeter City entertained Manchester United in the FA Cup Third Round on 4 January 1969, the programme notes said '... in the past we have seen ten First Division sides on this ground but never before have we had the privilege of welcoming such an illustrious side as Manchester United'. The writer had obviously forgotten this game on 19 October 1960 (only nine years earlier) when City and Manchester United met in the League Cup First Round during the competition's first season. The game ended in a 1-1 draw, with 16,000 people watching what was, of course, both clubs' first-ever League Cup game: this was 338 more than turned up at Old Trafford to see United win the replay 4-1.

Although there were only 15,662 at Old Trafford – where they are used to watching the best of English football – City fans had to exist on a more modest diet and were not going to turn down the chance of watching players like John Giles, Dennis Violet and Nobby Stiles. Another point of interest for the supporters was the return of Maurice Setters to St James's Park at right back for United.

A fair crowd in 'The Cowshed' watch a City practice match in August 1963. The game must have done the players some good as a few days later they began the promotion season with a 2-1 win at Valley Parade against Bradford City. 'The Cowshed' – a favourite haunt of many of Exeter City's noisiest and best-behaved followers – was built in 1925.

City did not have too many cup distractions during their 1963/64 promotion season. They went out of the League Cup 1-0 at Hull in the First Round. In the FA Cup, after beating Shrewsbury Town 2-1 at home, they lost 2-0 to Bristol City at St James's Park in front of 15,000 fans in the Second Round. Here, George Northcott gets in a header against Bristol City. It was his only season at St James's Park and, because Alan Banks was cup-tied with Cambridge City, he had the unusual record of playing in both FA Cup games whilst only having one League appearance against York City. He left for Cheltenham Town at the end of the season.

Brighton & Hove defender Dave Turner heads away in a City attack at St James's Park in 1963/64. Exeter's centre forward Adrian Thorne (9), who was actually born in Brighton, watches the action.

Dermot Curtis (9) in action against Shrewsbury at St James's Park in 1963/64. The press box was still standing, even if it appears to be no longer in use. Today the club's offices stand on this piece of waste ground.

A great favourite with fans during his five seasons with Exeter City, Dermot Curtis became the only Exeter City player to win an international cap while on the club's books when he played for the Republic of Ireland against Austria in 1964. Here, he scores one of his thirty-nine League and cup goals for City between 1963 and 1969.

Exeter City, 1963. From left to right, back row: Keith Harvey, Arnold Mitchell, John Henderson, Colin Tinsley, Cecil Smyth, Les MacDonald, Des Anderson. Front row: John McMillan, Barry Pierce, Eric Welsh, Ray Carter, Brian Jenkins.

Alan Banks, seen here trying to get a shot in, had two spells with Exeter City in the 1960s. A Liverpudlian, he played for them a while before joining Cambridge City. Banks cost City five thousand pounds in 1963/64, scoring eighteen goals in twenty-eight games in that first season. He left for Plymouth Argyle at the end of the 1965/66 season but was back a year later and became the first Exeter player to score 100 goals for the club and, in all, netted 107 times in his 271 games with The Grecians. He moved to Poole Town in 1973.

Another City player with a goal-scoring reputation was Fred Binney, a player who was cast in the mould of the old-fashioned centre forward who went in where it hurt looking for his goals. Here, he is bursting through for one of the ninety-eight goals he scored for Exeter. He joined the club from neighbouring Torquay United in 1968, scoring thirty-one goals in the 1973/74 season – his last before moving to Brighton & Hove Albion. Later, he joined Plymouth Argyle and the still-fairly-exclusive club of footballers who have turned out for Devon's three League sides.

Alan Banks where he liked to put the ball – in the back of the net! He scored twice in this game against Chesterfield in 1964 when City won 6-1. The other goals were scored by Dermot Curtis, Adrian Thorne (2) and Graham Rees.

Fred Binney (8) gets in a header against Crewe Alexandra, even if it looks more like John Giles (right) is getting his head to the ball. Barry Rowan is the man beside John Giles' knee. Fred did not score on this occasion, but Barry Rowan, Joe Gadstone and Alan Banks all found the net in a 3-1 City win.

FOOTBALL LEAGUE CUP, 3rd ROUND

TOTTENHAM HOTSPUR

v.

EXETER CITY

Official Programme

Price SIXPENCE

SEASON 1968–69   Wednesday, 25th Sept., 1968

Vol. 61   No. 11   KICK-OFF 7.30 p.m.

A lot of fans watched Exeter City's five League Cup games in 1968/69. In the First Round they drew 0-0 at Home Park in front of 8,662 fans. A second goal-less draw, this time after extra-time, attracted 13,338 to St James's Park with another 10,884 going to Plainmoor to watch City finally beat Argyle 1-0 (again after extra-time). In the Second Round, Sheffield Wednesday – going well in Division One at the time – came to Exeter and lost 3-1. There were 15,962 at that game and then another 25,796 watched Tottenham Hotspur beat Exeter City 6-3 at White Hart Lane in Round Three.

It is not all 10,000 plus gates if you are on Exeter City's books. Here, a handful of supporters watch John Neale score for the 'A' team against St Lukes College at the Cat & Fiddle training ground.

Exeter City, who had beaten Newport County 3-1 after a 0-0 draw at St James's Park and then Colchester United 1-0 away, landed Manchester United at home for the second time in nine years when the FA Cup Third Round draw was made. It was not surprising that 18,500 people watched the game on 4 January 1969 – it is not every day that players the calibre of Bobby Charlton, Nobby Stiles, Alex Stepney, Denis Law and George Best come to Exeter.

Manchester United, the European Cup holders, may well have won 3-1 by virtue of their second-half superiority. But they, especially keeper Alex Stepney, were surprised when Alan Banks (out of picture) put City ahead in the first half. John Corr wheels to join Banks in his celebrations.

Barnstaple-born John Neale is sent out as a substitute at Lincoln on 31 August 1974 by trainer Jack Edwards. He replaced Brian Joy. Something was certainly needed as City lost 5-0.

Exeter City, 1970/71. From left to right, back row: Keith Harvey, John Wingate, Brian Sharples, Jimmy Blain, Peter Shearing, Mike Balson, Bob Wilson, Graham Parker, Joe Gadston, John Newman. Front row: John Corr, Campbell Crawford, Alan Banks, Barry Rowan, John Mitten, John Giles, Steve Morris, Fred Binney.

Bobby Hodges tries to keep the ball in play during a FA Cup First Round game against Newport County at St James's Park on 1 November 1974. He may have succeeded but City still lost 2-1, despite later completing a Division Four double over the Welsh side.

In keeping with a game that ended 0-0, Peter Hatch's low header against Brentford on Boxing Day 1975 went wide. The other City players are: Alan Beer, John Templeman, Bobby Hodge, Nick Jennings, Bobby Saxton, -?-.

Above: Southport 'keeper John Coates is not amused as the ball, from a Lammie Robertson spot-kick, is about to cross the line. City won 3-1 at St James's Park on 30 October 1976, with Robertson claiming all three goals – two of them penalties. It was the Exeter skipper's first hat-trick in ten years of League football and the goals were his first of the season. Below: Tony Kellow is spreadeagled on the turf after the foul that brought the first of the penalties.

City's John Templeman (out of picture) has sent the Newport County goalkeeper the wrong way with this strike at St James's Park on 28 February 1976 while Alan Beer is following up. City won the match 3-1.

The 1976/77 season would see Exeter City finish second and win promotion to Division Three. Some of the players must have had a premonition: going up here before the season has even started are, from left to right: Peter Hatch, Keith Clapham, Alan Hooker, Graham Weeks, Richard Key and Bobby Saxton. Still with their feet on the ground are Tony Morrin, Mike Green, Harry Holman, Bobby Hodge and Alan Beer.

The full squad for that season are more restrained for the club's official pre-season *Express &
Echo* photograph. From left to right, back row: Peter Hatch, Bobby Saxton, Richard Key, Jack
Edwards (Trainer), Phil Howe, Tony Kellow, John Templeman. Middle row: Alan Hooker,
Alan Beer, Keith Clapham, John Newman (Manager), Tony Morrin, Nicky Jennings, John
Hore. Front row: Harry Holman, Bobby Hodge, Graham Weeks, Mike Green, Mike Jordan.

Well saved officer! Police Sergeant Peter Hinchcliffe brings the full weight of the law to bear on
this Huddersfield man after fighting broke out between rival supporters at Exeter coach station.
City had beaten the Yorkshire side 4-1 on 27 March 1976 with Alan Beer (2), Lammie
Robertson and Keith Bowker scoring for The Grecians.

Keith Bowker runs off the pitch after scoring City's second goal in a 2-0 win over Barnsley at St James's Park. Peter Hatch had scored the first goal. Looking back in despair is Barnsley keeper Peter Springett, the former Sheffield Wednesday favourite.

After a Tony Kellow goal gave them a 1-0 win at Home Park in a League Cup, First Round, first-leg game, Exeter City came back to St James's Park to again beat Plymouth Argyle 1-0. This time Mike Jordan was the scorer and he is seen here jumping to head the ball. Alan Beer (10) and Keith Clapham are the supporting City players with Bobby Hodge over on the right. The big clubs might tend to scorn this competition today, but in the 1970s it brought in useful revenue to clubs like Exeter City. At a time when City were averaging around 3,500 at home League games, the two League Cup fixtures attracted gates of 8,500 to Plymouth and 9,000 at Exeter.

This goal from Bobby Hodge (facing the camera) was the only one of the game against Colchester United at St James's Park on 12 February 1977, adding three more points to City's promotion bag. Tony Kellow (8) looks on as Hodge drives the ball between two Colchester defenders (3 and 5).

Exeter City show off their new first-team strip in February 1977. The shirts with the narrow stripes are in the club's traditional red and white livery while the wider-striped kit is the blue and white one, worn for away games. From left to right, back row: Harry Holman, Tony Morrin, Mike Jordan, Nicky Jennings, Tony Kellow. Middle row: John Hore (Captain), John Templeman, Mike Green, Phil Howe, Richard Key, Graham Weeks, Keith Clapham, Alan Hooker. Front row: Lammie Robertson, Alan Beer, Bobby Saxton (Player/Manager), Bobby Hodge, Peter Hatch.

Barnsley lost 1-0 at St James's Park on 8 January 1977. Here, Tony Kellow is putting a shot past Peter Springett, in goal for the northern club. However, the 'keeper was not unduly worried as the ball missed the post.

Another win for City during the run-in to promotion in April 1977, as they beat Southend United 3-1 at St James's Park. Player/manager Bobby Saxton heads the third goal.

Tony Kellow, with Lammie Robertson looking on, goes in against Southend United. Kellow, Alan Beer and Bobby Saxton all scored in a 3-1 victory – the second of eleven wins in the last thirteen games of the season.

Some of the 6,722 gate at St James's Park cheer with relief at Alan Beer's late-late, only-goal-of-the-game winner against Darlington on 30 April 1977. From this point only games against Barnsley, Doncaster Rovers and Aldershot stood between Exeter City and promotion.

90

City's match programme for the visit of Aldershot says it all: 'We're Up'. A 3-0 win at Doncaster the previous Saturday had made certain that The Grecians could not be caught by fifth-placed Swansea. Another 3-0 win in this, the Aldershot game, saw them promoted as runners-up, the first time they had finished in second place since 1932/33. The programme struck one sour note. 'Our gates have been disappointing, nowhere near the 1963/64 [the previous promotion season] average of 7,500'. However, as the programme went on to state, 'Who cares?' (apart from the bank manager maybe)!

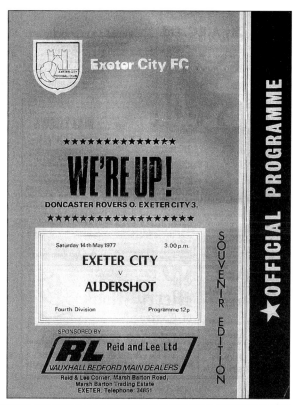

The celebrations began immediately after the game, with the City players joining the fans in the stand where trainer Jack Edwards is about to get a champagne ducking from Alan Beer. The other players are Graham Weeks (with bottle), Alan Beer and Tony Kellow.

The champagne continued to flow in the dressing room afterwards. From left to right, at the back are: Tony Long (Physiotherapist), John Baugh, Lammie Roberston and Alan Beer. In front: Bobby Saxton, Mike Green, Chris Howes (Club Photographer) John Hore, Bobby Hodge, Tony Kellow, Peter Hatch, Richard Key, John Templeman, Graham Weeks and Nicky Jennings.

A few days later the players did a 'lap of honour' through the city and cheering crowds before arriving at the Guildhall for a civic reception. On the open-top double-decker are John Baugh, Bobby Hodge, Phil Howe, John Templeman, Graham Weeks and Richard Key.

Exeter's fourteenth-century Guildhall has gazed down on much of the city's splendid history. Henry VII came here in person to say 'Thank you' to the citizens for driving out the imposter Perkin Warbeck in 1497. However, it is doubtful whether he was greeted with as much enthusiasm as City's player/manager Bobby Saxton was here when he acknowledged the crowd's applause from the Guildhall balcony, after thanking them for their support during the season. Saxton, who joined Exeter from Plymouth Argyle as a player and succeeded John Newman as manager, could probably have taken Exeter even further. But he went back to Plymouth as manager before leaving them, after only twelve months, for Blackburn Rovers and a bigger salary.

It was one crowd the police were happy to see and, as is usual with Exeter City fans, they all behaved themselves. Looking up at the cameraman are Clifford Hill, Ray Ellis (Promotion Manager), John Baugh, Bobby Hodge, Phil Howe, John Templeman, Graham Weeks and Richard Key.

The 1976/77 promotion team. From left to right, back row: Alan Beer, John Templeman, Lammie Robertson, Nicky Jennings. Middle row: Graham Weeks, Peter Hatch, Richard Key, Bobby Hodge. Front row: Tony Kellow, John Hore, Jack Edwards (Trainer), Bobby Saxton.

Lammie Robertson watches as Bobby Hodge goes close with a header against Barnsley at St James's Park in the mid 1970s.

It may not match the palatial halls of Highbury, Pride Park or the other St James's Park at Newcastle, but Exeter City's home is just that – home and even homely to its dedicated band of loyal supporters. There were over 6,000 of them here to see their team beat Colchester 1-0 on a cold February day. In the Middle Ages, St James's belonged to the poor of St Stephen's parish. Mention is made in the nineteenth century of a touring managerie using the space once a year; the rest of the time it was used for fattening pigs. Then the 1904 lease stipulated no more manageries, shows, circuses or steam roundabouts. Henry Duke, the city's MP, intervened in 1911 when landowners refused to release the neighbouring ground needed to enlarge the playing area which was too small to stage FA Cup games (Exeter either conceded home advantage or played at the County Ground). He paid for the stand to be made larger and for extra standing accommodation and for many years the Big Bank was known as the Duke Bank. 'The Cowshed' was built in 1925 but the whole ground was in danger in 1969 when the City Council planned to build a new road system through the pitch. Happily, this never came about.

Sadly, Newport County are no longer a league side. But perhaps they might still have been be if they had always had crowds similar to that of the 3,500 watching Exeter City win 3-0 at Somerton Park in 1977. In this picture, City's Nicky Jennings watches the 'keeper clear.

Mr Hunting is having none of it as Nicky Jennings protests that he ought to have played the advantage rule when Alan Beer netted at Belle Vue against Doncaster Rovers. The official had already blown for the infringement on Jennings. Lammie Robertson (9) looks to the crowd in disbelief. Still, Exeter did win 3-0 in the end, with Beer taking two of the goals.

Exeter finished down in seventeenth position in 1977/78 – their first season back in the Division Three. From left to right, back row: Tony Long (Physiotherapist), Brian Clarke, John Templeman, Steve Nute, Vincent O'Keefe, Richard Key, Jimmy Giles. Harry Holman, Bobby Hodge, Peter Hatch, Jack Edwards (Trainer). Middle row: Lee Roberts, Fred Ingham, John Delve, Colin Randell, Bobby Saxton (Player/Manager), John Hore (Captain), Keith Bowker, Tony Kellow, Tony Mitchell. Front row: Dick Forbes, Paul Smythe, Roy Ireland, Colin Bickley.

Exeter, after wins over Newport County (4-2 after a 1-1 draw away) and Minehead (3-0 away) in the FA Cup were drawn at home to Wolverhampton Wanderers in the Third Round in 1977/78. City's player/manager Bobby Saxton wrote in the match programme for the Wolverhampton game that it was '...his sincere hope that the excitement and magic that such matches bring will keep you on the edge of your seats for the full ninety minutes...'. This one did – but maybe not for the reasons he expected.

It should have been a lucrative time for Exeter City, as there were 14,377 people in St James's Park to see the Division One side lucky to escape with a 2-2 draw (they won the replay at Molineux 3-1). However, the visiting fans were guilty of disgraceful behaviour, causing around £5,000 of damage. In this picture they have flattened the fence behind the goal at the St James's Road End and the police are powerless to stop them invading the pitch. Other damage included a crossbar broken after the match and mindless grafitti on most walls between the ground and the coach park. That many of the Wolves' fans had come looking for trouble cannot be denied: some of those seen here are hooded.

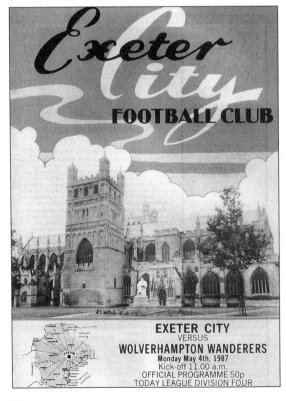

Sic transit gloria mundi. Wolverhampton Wanderers, Division One Champions three times, runners-up five times, Division Two champions twice, FA Cup winners four times, runners-up four times and UEFA Cup and League Cup winners, went back to St James's Park nine years after the infamous FA Cup game as a Division Four side. For the Cup match, City had played: Richard Key, John Templeman, Peter Hatch, Keith Bowker, Jimmy Giles, Bobby Saxton, Colin Randell, Tony Kellow, Harry Holman, Lee Roberts and John Hore. Nine years later, only Tony Kellow remained with City and he had twice left the club and was now in last season with them – this would be his penultimate game for Exeter. In this match he scored the last of his club-record 162 goals with a penalty that had to be taken twice. He later missed another penalty.

Some of the players meet their new manager, Welsh international Brian Godfrey, who joined Exeter City in January 1979. He had previously played for Everton, Scunthorpe, Preston North End, Aston Villa, Bristol Rovers and Newport County, before becoming the manager at Bath City, the club he returned to when he left St James's Park in 1983. Wally Rice (Vice-chairman), Lee Roberts, John Hore (Captain), Peter Hatch and Jimmy Giles are standing behind the manager.

Brian Godfrey decides to take his own team shots at the start of the 1979/80 season. From left to right, back row: Vince O'Keefe, Steve Nute, Ian Main, Dave Pullar, Peter Hatch, Phil Roberts, Martin Rogers. Middle row: Keith Bowker, John Hore, Roy Ireland, Ian Pearson. Front row: -?-, -?-.

Ian Pearson jumps up, only to head a Steve Neville cross wide during a 1-1 draw with Rotherham United at St James's Park on 1 December 1979.

Yellow this time as Peter Rogers goes down clutching at his ankle. This tackle by Sheffield United defender Paul Gardner led to the player's name going into Alan Robinson's little book at St James's Park in 1979.

Exeter City's last big moment of the 1970s saw them travel to play Liverpool at Anfield for a League Cup, Fourth Round tie, after they had knocked out Hereford United (5-2 on aggregate), Doncaster Rovers (6-4 on aggregate) and Birmingham City (2-1 away). A lot of City fans made the 470 mile round trip, including the chairman, Gerald Vanstone, and the other directors (above), as well as the players' wives and girlfriends, with Sue Hore, the wife of the captain, holding a special mascot (below).

Exeter City forward Ian Pearson beats Liverpool's England international goalkeeper Ray
Clemence two minutes from the end of their cup game at Anfield. Unfortunately, it did not
count as the referee had already blown for offside and Liverpool won 2-0. Although there were
only 21,000 people at the game, there were enough fans on the famous Kop to give Exeter a
standing ovation after the match.

Not all Liverpool supporters were as welcoming. Here, Glen Ponsford, a director of Glenline
Coaches, removes pieces of glass shattered by missiles thrown at the coach as it left Liverpool.

Five
Modern Ups and Downs

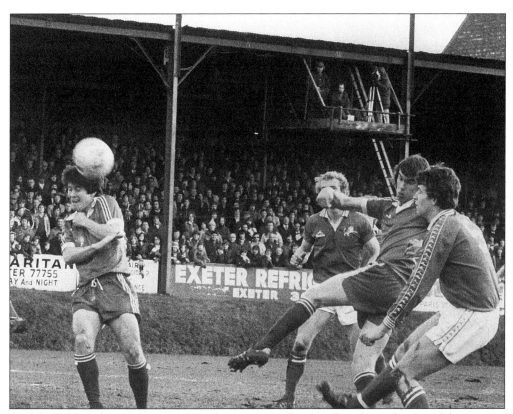

Andy Bell (dark shorts) from South Petherton gets in his first shot during his City debut against Millwall at St James's Park on 2 February 1980. He missed but City went on to win 2-1. Peter Rogers ducks as the ball flies past him.

In 1980/81, Exeter City began the new decade by reaching the Sixth Round of the FA Cup for the first time since the epic run of 1930/31 – half a century earlier. They got rid of Leatherhead (5-0 home), Millwall (1-0 away), Maidstone United (4-2 away) and then, on 24 January 1981, they went to Filbert Street to draw 1-1 with Leicester City. Twenty-four hours before the replay at St James's Park, the City players learnt that, if they beat Leicester, the Fifth Round draw had sent them to the other St James's Park in the Football League, the home of – then Division Two – Newcastle United. Above: skipper John Delve, on the left at the back, expresses what are probably the true feelings of the team. The players standing are: John Delve, Dave Pullar, Peter Hatch, Ian Pearson, Tony Kellow, Martin Rogers, Dick Forbes, Steve Nute, Lee Roberts, Roy Ireland. On the ground are Phil Roberts and Peter Rogers. Below: fans applauding after the draw at Leicester in the first game.

Fans queuing for tickets to see the replay. The Grecians won the game splendidly with an excellent Tony Kellow hat-trick. The attendance was given as 21,000 which, if this was accurate, is sixteen more were at the Sunderland replay back in 1931 – a figure always quoted as the record gate at St James's Park.

And the fans did Exeter proud again with their support at Newcastle's St James's Park, where Lee Roberts scored the goal that gave City a 1-1 draw in front of 37,420 people.

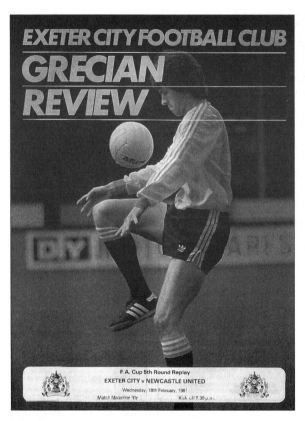

The team repaid the fans' loyalty with a stunning 4-0 win back at their own St James's Park the following Wednesday in front of 17,668 people. The Magpies made the long, 730 mile round trip to find themselves three goals down at the interval and knocked out of cup competitions for the fourth time in four years by a Division Three side. Peter Hatch, Ian Pearson, Philip Roberts and Peter Rogers scored for Exeter.

Fans queue for tickets for the Newcastle FA Cup replay.

City's cup dreams were ended 2-0 at White Hart Lane in front of a 41,000 gate. Above: Garth Crooks bursts through the City defence chased by Phil Roberts, Lee Roberts, John Delve and Peter Hatch. Below: Graham Roberts, later to come to the West Country as Yeovil Town's player/manager, climbs above John Delve to clear.

It was not all cup glory for Exeter City in the early 1980s. In 1981/82, after beating Cardiff City 4-3 on aggregate in the First Round of the League Cup, they were soundly thrashed by Liverpool, who won 5-0 at Anfield and then 6-0 in the second leg at St James's Park. At the Park, the 11,700 gate was 700 more than the game at Liverpool. Above: Kenny Dalglish outpaces Lee Roberts and John Delve at Anfield. Below: any faint hopes Exeter City may had had about pulling back the five-goal deficit were ended in the fifteenth minute when Ian Rush beat Len Bond for the first of the six goals.

Tony Kellow scored both City goals in a 2-0 win over Walsall in 1982. The Rogers cousins, Peter and Martin, join him in celebrating the first. Kellow played in all of City's League games that season, scoring twenty-one goals.

Steve Neville tries, unsuccessfully, to find a way through the Leyton Orient defence at St James's Park in November 1982. Peter Rogers is on the left.

City players raise their glasses to toast Paul Sandle and Bob Palmer at the official opening of the Near Post video shop in Black Boy Road during November 1982. The soccer stars were regular visitors to the Near Post, which was for many years the official souvenir shop of Exeter City Football Club, but is now closed and there is a club shop on the ground.

Exeter City just escaped relegation to Division Four at the end of the 1982/83 season, finishing in nineteenth place courtesy of a 1-1 draw away to Newport County on the last day of the season. It might be raining but City players are happy as they celebrate at the end of the game.

Former England international and captain Gerry Francis arrived at St James's Park in July 1983 as manager to replace Brian Godfrey, soon after City had narrowly escaped relegation. He stayed less than a year and this time City were relegated after finishing bottom. All this was far from the new manager's mind when he lined up with the players for this team shot in August 1983. From left to right, back row: Martin Rogers, Ray Pratt, Nicky Marker, Graham Kirkup, -?-, Tony Kellow. Middle row: Martin Ling, Darren Clifford, Symon Burgher, Len Bond, -?-, Mike Lane, -?-, Malcolm Musgrove. Front row: Dick Forbes, Tony Dennis, Dave Harle, Gerry Francis, Keith Viney, Peter Rogers, Steve Neville.

Steve Neville raises his hands to salute the Popular End fans after scoring City's third goal in a 3-2 win over Millwall. Ray Pratt (9) and Peter Rogers are turning away. There are big gaps in the crowd as only 2,859 fans watched the game. The gates did not improve as City only won two of their remaining twenty-seven matches.

City's new signing Trevor Morgan from Bristol City finds himself on all fours as Crewe goalkeeper Brian Parkin cuts out a high cross meant for Nicky Marker (5). Crewe won 2-0.

City might be on the way down at this time but there was still nearly 7,000 people at St James's Park to see them draw 1-1 with the 'Old Enemy' Plymouth Argyle in April 1984. This was the only League match that stand-in 'keeper Richard Crabtree – making the save in the picture – played for The Grecians.

Jim McNichol's powerful header was cleared off the line by Rochdale defender Mike Fielding, who was thought by most people in St James's Park – especially John Sims and Ray Pratt to the right of the picture – to have handled the ball. If this was the case, he robbed City of two points, as the game ended as a 1-1 draw.

This man came to watch a football match and he was not going to be distracted by the police when they ejected an unruly fan from the grandstand after disturbances in City's last home game of the 1983/84 season. If he was a City fan then Bournemouth spoilt his day as they won 2-0.

Grecian defender Frank Howarth goes off on a stretcher during City's 1-1 draw with near neighbours Torquay United on Boxing Day 1984. Keith Viney and Danny O'Shea give the St John's Ambulance men a helping hand.

England manager Bobby Robson unveils the plaque to officially open 'The Cowshed' at St James's Park after its £100,000 refurbishment. With him, attending City's game against Southend United, is club chairman Mr Ivor Doble. The game ended a goal-less draw, the second of four successive Exeter games to end that way. In all Exeter would draw twenty-three of their forty-six League games that season, equalling the League record set by Norwich City.

The 1985/86 playing staff. From left to right, back row: Simon Rawlins, Scott Hiley, Ian Dobson, Clive Nelson, Jamie Harris, Richard Massey, Warren Hadley, Craig Horton, Richard Hancock, Mark Robson, Lee Lorimer. Middle row: Mike Radford (Youth Development Officer), Mark Walsh, Darren Gale, Jim McNichol, Alden McCaffery, John Shaw, Nick Marker, Keith Viney, Graeme Kirkup, Phil King, Colin Appleton (Manager). Front row: Martin Ling, Ray Pratt, Tony Kellow, Trevor Morgan, Tony Evans, Steve Harrower, Alan Crawford.

Wolves at St James's Park again and memories went back to 1977/78 (see p. 98) when the Midland club's fans caused disturbances. Thankfully, there was not the same damage on this occasion, a 3-1 Wanderers victory on 4 May 1987, thanks to firm action by the police.

Champions at last! Tom Kelly holds the Division Four trophy aloft at the home game with Burnley on 1 May 1990. Dave Walter, Richard Young, Brian McDermott and Shaun Taylor join in the celebrations.

The forging of Exeter City's Division Four Championship in 1989/90 began two years earlier when former Leeds and England star Terry Cooper was sacked by Bristol City. He accepted the offer of the manager's job at St James's Park and steered City, twenty-second in 1987/88, into tenth place. A year later they were champions and presented with the trophy at their last home game of the season, in which City beat Burnley 2-1. Four days later they ended their season in style, winning 5-1 at Lincoln.

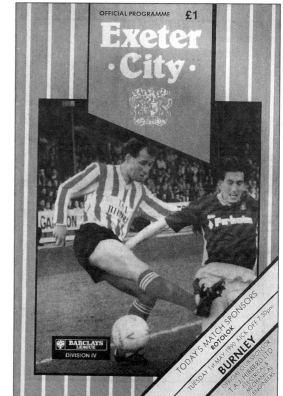

The champions on their open-top bus tour of Exeter with -?-, -?-, Stuart Smith, Danny Bailey, Kevin Miller, Shaun Taylor (with trophy) and the *Express & Echo* photographer looking down from the bus.

Manager Terry Cooper was rewarded for winning promotion and the Division Four title with a new contract, which he is pictured here signing on 30 May, watched by club chairman Ivor Doble.

City were rewarded with a £25,000 sponsorship deal from Barclays' Bank, whose director of personnel, Bob Gordon (left), presented the cheque to City chairman Ivor Doble. The Football League's finance officer, Bob Gordon, is not smiling – perhaps because Ivor Doble and Terry Cooper have collared the bubbly stuff?

City skipper Shaun Taylor loses out to the Reading defenders in 1990.

New signing Gordon Hobson scores in the same game, which Reading won 3-1. He came from Lincoln City for £20,000 after a tribunal fixed the fee. City wanted to pay £10,000, Lincoln wanted to get £100,000 for the player.

Trouble flared outside St James's Park in August 1990 when City and Swansea fans clashed after the game, which Exeter City won 2-0.

Police reinforcements rush to the scene as the fans, on their way home after the game, part to let them through.

One of the unhappier developments of the modern game is shirt tugging which, sadly, goes mostly unchecked by referees. The victim here is City skipper Shaun Taylor, who has clearly been fouled in the Tranmere penalty area. 'Play on' was the referee's verdict.

Birmingham City player John Gayle (on the ground) clears in a crowded goalmouth. The City man who is helping to cause the panic is Steve Neville. It was quite a game for Birmingham's Gayle, who had cost the Midland club £175,000 when he moved from Wimbledon some three months earlier. He scored both their goals in a 2-0 win in front of just over 5,000 fans. For Exeter it was the first of a run of five games that brought only one goal and no points.

The *Express & Echo* photograph of Exeter City at the start of the 1991/92 season. From left to right, back row: Jon Brown, Kevin Maloy, David Cole, Kevin Miller, Scott Daniels. Second row: Mike Davenport (Physiotherapist), Gordon Hobson, Gary Marshall, Steve O'Shaughnessy, David Cooper, Chris O'Donnell, Tony Frankland, Graham Waters, Mike Radford (Youth Development Officer). Third row: Scott Hiley, Steve Moran, Mark Cooper, Alan Ball (Manager), Steve Williams, Darren Rowbotham, Tom Kelly. Front row: Glenn Sprod, Mark Brown, Neil Fairchild, Zac Locke, Craig Taylor, Toby Redwood.

Steve Moran's low cross fails to find any City colleague against Stoke in 1991.

The City squad, complete with bikes supplied by Kings of Wellington, about to set off on a cross-country ride under the guidance of two Royal Marine instructors in order to get fit for the 1992/93 season.

Further training for the 1992/93 season sees the City players at the Cat and Fiddle training ground.

The 1992/93 season squad. From left to right, back row: Steve Allen, Mark Hutchings, Scott Daniels, Kevin Maloy, Kevin Miller, Eamonn Dolan, Richard Pears, Phil Lafferty. Second row: Mike Chapman (Physiotherapist), George Kent (Community Liaison Officer), Alan Tonge, Gary Chapman, David Cooper, Gary Marshall, Toby Redwood, Jon Brown, Craig Taylor, Tom Kelly, Eamonn Collins, Mike Radford (Youth Development Officer), Alan Ball (Manager). Third row: Andy Cook, Steve Moran, Scott Hiley, Peter Whiston, Steve Williams (Assistant Manager), Glenn Sprod, Andy Harris, John Hodge. Front: Mark Brown, Anthony Thirlby, Martin Phillips, Kevin Darch, Marc Baines, Jimmy Ball, Gary Rice, Matthew Harris.

Ronnie Jepson (9) celebrates after scoring against Stoke City in 1992/93. Joining in are John Hodge, Andy Harris and Eamonn Collins.

Exeter City skipper Shaun Taylor in action against Bradford City in the 1990s.

Referee M. Bodenham looks at his watch as he makes his way off the pitch after the floodlights failed six minutes from time with Exeter losing 2-1 to Swansea City in a Second Round FA Cup match in December 1992. Justice was done as Swansea won the replayed game 4-1. By a strange coincidence, Mr Bodenham was in charge at Bristol City's Ashton Gate ground when their lights failed in the same season.

Scott Hiley, who did not handle the ball, clears under pressure against Swindon in 1993. Watching are Peter Whiston, Tom Kelly and John Hodge.

Something is making the players laugh during training at the Exeter Arena in July 1993.

Manager Peter Fox, just voted Player of the Year at the end of the 1993/94 season, looks to what promises to be an successful time ahead for Exeter City – even if he has just been bombarded by some Exeter College students in a penalty shoot-out challenge.

They also serve who only stand and wait – 'Your programme, sir?' – Dave Fisher, half of the authorship team for this book, has helped Exeter City as a programme seller since 1972. He has followed them since 1963 and, needless to say, is an avid collector of City programmes.

Acknowledgements

Much of the material used in this book came from Dave Fisher's personal and extensive collection of Exeter City memorabilia. As much again came from the archives of the *Express & Echo*, who have faithfully chronicled the Exeter City story since the club was formed in 1904. We must thank its Editor, Steve Hall, as well as Simon Carter of the sports desk and Sports Editor Jerry Charge for his introduction.

Others who have allowed us to use their own material are Paul Davy, Malcolm MacDonald – whose collection of over 600 City programmes made interesting reading and were an invaluable source of information – and Derek Warren who, nearly half a century later, still proudly keeps his own collection of pictures, cuttings and the match programmes from the games he played for Exeter City and Yeovil Town.

Barbara Sawicka and Anna Fitzsimmons, Reg Clarke's great-nieces, very kindly allowed us to use items from Nobby's much-cherished scrapbook. It was very useful to be able to check many statistics by referring to *Exeter City, A Complete Record 1904-1990*, a joint effort by Maurice Golesworthy, Garth Dykes and the late Alex Wilson. In a different direction we must thank the staff at Tempus Publishing, especially James Howarth, for help and encouragement. Last, but not least, we must thank Exeter City Football Club – without them this book could not have been written – and not forgetting manager Peter Fox, for his excellent foreword.